THE POWER OF POSITIVE ENERGY

HOW TO DECLUTTER YOUR MIND,
CONTROL EMOTIONS, MANAGE
STRESS, AND REWIRE YOUR BRAIN
BY LETTING GO OF WORRY AND
ANXIETY

VISHAL PANDEY

TABLE OF CONTENTS

Introduction

Greetings, I am Vishal, author of "*The Power of Positive Energy*," and I would like to thank you for purchasing this book.

My sole purpose for writing this book is to help people who are overwhelmed with negative thoughts shift to a more optimistic, positive thinking mindset to attain happiness and fulfillment in life.

I still remember reading about the importance of positive thinking and thinking - "I know all this."

But in my mind, I didn't give too much thought to it.

Now, after thirteen years of massive highs and lows, I am completely convinced that positive thinking is everything. Every action we take is determined by our thoughts. Positive thoughts reinforce positive actions, which move you in the right direction, while negative thoughts do the opposite.

In this book, we will cover the reasons behind your thoughts and how to change them and live positively every day.

Thoughts are powerful. A small positive thought in the morning can transform your entire day. If you realized how powerful your thoughts are, you'd never think a negative thought again.

I love this verse from the Bible: "As a man thinketh in his heart, so is he." You become what you think about. Ask yourself, "Do I think positively or not?"

Studies show that most of your thoughts are subconscious. They are habitual. We have been conditioned to think a certain way.

While media does play a role in forming our thinking habits, it begins when we were teeny-tiny versions of ourselves.

An average toddler hears the word "no" an astonishing 400 times in a day from parents, according to experts. 400 times in one day! A child's mind is like a sponge. It (eventually) learns to automatically expect more no's instead of yes. It slowly becomes a habit and gets stronger over time. Till the time you reach the age of 16, your mind has already become habitual of expecting more no's.

In all those early years, our life script was formed. While we were still learning to cope with the world, our elders dictated what was wrong and what was right. And whatever we did, we mostly got a 'no' for it. Whenever we messed up, we got reminded of how dumb we are. We listened to the people around us and took their advice to heart.

It all leads to the creation of a negative thinking habit, which is further accentuated by other external influences like social media and news channels.

Your brain behaves like a computer. The programs you put in get processed and determine what results you get. Similarly, the thoughts we put in our minds determine our words, feelings & actions.

Law of Attraction says, "Your thoughts become things." Your thoughts attract situations, people, and events in your life.

It is unlimited what the universe can bring when you understand the great secret that your thoughts become things.

Have you ever received a call from an old friend which you have not seen for a while but you were thinking about them?

This is the law of attraction in action.

Whatever you focus on, think about, read about, and talk about intensely, you are going to attract more of into your life. If we focus on the positive, we will attract positive people and events in your life. It's true for the opposite side as well.

In "*The Power of Positive Energy,*" we are going to cover:

* The way our mind works

* How to develop the habit of positive thinking

* How to boost your self-confidence and beliefs

* How to get motivated when you don't feel like it

* How to manifest the life you want

* How to be thankful for what you have

* How to forgive those who have wronged you in the past and attain inner peace

* How to live a healthy lifestyle that empowers you

* How to live a life full of joy, optimism, and inspiration

The advice and exercises coming up are powerful, and it's up to you to take this knowledge and use it. Remember: without its application, knowledge has no value. But when acted upon, it has the power to shape our destiny.

I wish you the best.

Positive Energy Principle #1

POSITIVE THINKING - 7 EXCELLENT WAYS TO INCREASE YOUR POSITIVITY

I was fighting with negative thoughts, depression, self-doubt, and procrastination for thirteen long years.

It was one of the most difficult times of my life. The struggle was real.

But I was determined to break out of my old mindset. I read every book and attended every seminar that I could find. I implemented every advice, method, and technique which made sense to me, and finally, after all those years, I did manage to break out of it.

I shared what I found with other people, and they experienced changes in their thoughts and behavior. I am confident that if you follow the advice coming up, you can drastically increase your positivity.

7 Excellent ways to increase your positivity

1. Seek the company of positive people

People – who you surround yourself with – have a TREMENDOUS effect on your mind. It's a well-known psychological fact that your thoughts and behavior are the combinations of personalities of five people you spend the most time with. These 'five people' can be real people – friends, family, coworkers... or influences – books, television, internet sites, newspapers, etc.

Your mind is very receptive. It learns fast! These influences can be very beneficial or very harmful to you. If you spend most of your time among negative people, you would never feel happy or confident. If your friends always whine and complain about things, you would end being a complainer as well.

Let me share a personal experience... Some time back, I landed a nice paying job in a good company. I thought everything was great. The atmosphere was good, the people were friendly, and the work profile was great. During the same period, I wanted to start an online business and was working on my blog.

My office hours, fortunately, gave me time to work on my online business, but... I did nothing. I didn't take any action despite all the free time I had. I always found some 'excuse' to delay the work.

As time passed, I started feeling bad for ignoring my heart's calling.

Soon, self-pity increased to a point where I couldn't take it anymore. I decided to figure out what was preventing me from taking action. For the next ten days, I observed my behavior very carefully and found that I had developed a crazy habit of making excuses.

I was not only avoiding my online business but also putting off office work and daily household chores.

It was unnatural for me because I never shied away from doing work. When did I start behaving like this? How did I form this habit?

I looked around and found that five of my teammates at the office were always trying to keep the workload as low as possible. They dreaded the thought of being burdened by work and were always making excuses to avoid it.

On an average day, I worked with them for the majority of my eight-hour job. My mind automatically picked up their excuse-making habit.

The power of social influence is astounding.

Constant, repeated statements from surrounding people have the power to brainwash you. For example, a person who grew up in a family where people always say "money doesn't grow on trees" or "rich people are greedy" will not have a very healthy relationship with money.

Be mindful when selecting people to spend time with. You will unknowingly CATCH their habits, thinking, behavior, talking & dressing style. You will become LIKE them.

2. Read Books, videos, audiobooks by people you admire

Just now, we discussed that we should spend most of our time in the company of positive, successful people. But what if we don't have anyone like that in our current social circle? What do we do then?

Here's the good news - positive influence doesn't need actual people themselves. It can be their books, audiobooks, videos, movies, songs... It all counts. Now you don't have an excuse to say, "but I don't have resources to go and meet all those successful people."

Find people you admire and read their books, watch their videos, listen to their tapes... you will automatically internalize their thinking and behavior.

Read their books, watch their videos...

It all counts in changing our mindset to a positive one.

Good self-help books & autobiographies can be incredibly helpful. A person, who went through various hardships all his life, decides to put down all that knowledge in an easy-to-read book... That's called a real opportunity. You can learn what he learned and use it whenever you face a similar situation.

Walt Disney said, "There is more treasure in books than in all the pirate's loot on Treasure Island."

Reading increases your creativity, expands your mind, and shows you that nothing is impossible in this world. By reading, you develop a new perspective over a thing you've known or how different actions lead to different results.

Books are beyond imagination. It's like a huge spider web, where you keep linking to more and more to things you knew and things you just learn, structuring new solutions and answers.

As you continue to indulge yourself in positive influence, you will discover that you tend to think more positive thoughts during the day.

3. Positive self-talk

Positive self-talk is the key to any successful person. If you can change the voice in your head, you can do anything.

Many studies have shown that the human brain can change itself well into the later years of adulthood. This phenomenon is called Neuro-Plasticity.

Every thought we think, every conscious or subconscious thought we say to ourselves, is translated into electrical signals which, in turn, control the emotions we feel, the words we say, and the actions we take.

We program our brain with our self-talk.

It is the language of the brain.

Thus, self-talk also provides an opportunity to override our past negative programming by using repetition.

So how do we do it? How can we use self-talk to change the non-stop conversation going inside our heads?

The answer is simple - we use the right language.

Using positive and present-tense statements like "I am..." or "right now, I accept..." or "I am becoming..." emphasizes changes happening at the present moment. Not in the distant future. Your mind takes it wayyy more seriously than using future statements like "I will be happy" or "I will be successful."

For example, say, "I am going to become a good person." notice how that feels.

Not very inspiring, eh?

Now say, "I am a good person."

How did that feel?

You can re-wire your brain profoundly by using positive, present-tense statements daily. Change the old, unhealthy self-talk with a positive one and repeat it whenever you find a few seconds of free time.

Some of my personal favorite self-talk affirmations are:

"I am enough."

"I can do it."

"God is always with me."

"I am a winner."

"Today is my day."

"I deserve the best, and I do my best."

"I forgive myself."

"I deeply and completely, love and accept myself."

"I am worthy of being loved just the way I am."

"All I seek is already within me."

"I am so grateful that money comes to me in increasing quantities, from multiple sources."

"I am becoming healthier every day. All is well."

Repeating these self-talk affirmations created a huge positive influence in my life and in the lives of people I shared them with. You can adopt these as well, or you can create new ones that suit your particular needs.

If you are going to create new ones yourself, make sure they are positive and in the present tense.

4. Smile and laugh more often

Smiling and laughter are the opposite of feeling bad or negative. Just by adopting this new habit in your life, you cannot help but feel good and positive.

The body and mind are interconnected. The way we use the body affects our thoughts and feelings.

A smile - even a forced one - will make you feel happier instantly. This is a great way to lift your mood and spread positivity to those around you.

Try this exercise. Stand in front of your mirror, look at yourself and force out a smile or laughter.

You can force a smile, or you can think of a person, child, pet, situation, or anything that makes you smile. Either one of them will work very well.

It immediately fills you up with positive feelings. Keep it up, and you won't be able to stop smiling.

Go try it right now.

While doing this exercise, I always end up laughing. I feel very positive as well...You can do the same!

Science says laughter and smiling can cure diseases and depression!

Smile and laugh more often. It will increase the positive energy in your day and spread outward to the people around you. It's a win-win for everyone.

5. Exercise

Only a healthy body can sustain a healthy mind.

Exercise not only changes your body, but it also changes your mood.

Physical movement increases blood flow to all parts of the body, including the brain. It causes an increased supply of oxygen and nutrients, which serve as fuel for the brain. A plethora of hormones are released that play a part in sharpening cognitive functions in the brain:

* **Endorphins** reduce stress and help you relax. As a direct result, they help fight anxiety and depression. They also reduce pain & discomfort and enhance pleasure & improve self-esteem.

* **Serotonin** regulates your hunger, makes you sleep better, and influences your mood. All of these go hand-in-hand to make us feel happier, relaxed, and positive.

* **Dopamine** signals reward and pleasure centers in our brain. It controls our motivation levels and thus, determines how much action we take towards our goals.

* **Testosterone** is important for both men and women. It regulates your metabolism, muscle growth, and sexual drive. Low levels of testosterone may cause depression and obesity.

In a recent study done by the department of exercise science at the University of Georgia, it was found that even exercising for 20 minutes leads to increased information processing and happiness.

What it means is, if you keep chilling out on your sofa all day, you are not giving your brain a chance to operate at its full potential.

I highly recommend taking a minimum of 30 minutes daily for physical activity - walking, jogging, cycling, weightlifting, cardio, yoga, tai-chi - select anyone you like. Do check with your doctor before starting.

In addition to the above morning exercise, get up from your chair every 30 minutes to stretch your legs. Take a short walk around the office. Go to the water cooler, take a sip and come back. Just get up and move around a bit.

Try doing both of these for ten days. You will notice a substantial improvement in your positivity and energy levels. Physical exercise refreshes the mind & body and adds more 'life' to your day.

6. Meditation

Thousands of years ago, Buddha said – *"Thoughts are the cause of all suffering."*

We are consumed with thinking all day long. We can never completely stop thinking. Even if you consciously try to get rid of all the thoughts, it will not work. In the Buddhist culture, this is called the 'monkey brain.' Our thoughts and attention wander like crazy.

To attain peace and happiness, we have to take control of our minds. The ultimate freedom is freedom from thoughts.

Suppose you are trying to have a happy, carefree conversation with your partner at home, and your mind is wondering about the project report you have to complete tomorrow before lunch. How effective would that conversation be?

Benefits of meditation

Meditation trains the mind to be in the present moment, which empowers us to lead a happier life and to cope with any difficulties we face. Research shows that meditation is an effective therapy for many common diseases and increases happiness, empathy, and compassion for others.

People who meditate also experience lower levels of anxiety, anger, mental stress, and an increase in presence, positivity, and peace of mind. Meditation can be a supportive practice for those who have experienced trauma.

The effortless meditation practice

a) Set an alarm for 10-15 minutes.

b) Sit comfortably on a chair, keeping your back relaxed & upright

c) Close your eyes and start noticing your breath coming in and out. Notice everything about it: when it enters your nostrils to when it goes in your diaphragm. The movement of your stomach going up and down, etc.

d) Eventually, your mind will start thinking about something. You will get lost in your thoughts. You lose focus on your breath and start dwelling on the thought itself. It's Ok. Whenever you catch yourself focusing on your thoughts instead of being aware of your breath, gently and calmly shift your focus to your breath.

f) What will certainly happen is you will lose your focus again and get lost in thoughts. Again, simply shift your focus to your breath calmly.

g) Keep doing this till your alarm goes off.

This simple exercise will improve the overall state of your mind (i.e., Peace, positivity, clarity of thoughts, concentration, willpower, focus) by a large margin. Its effectiveness has been proven in researches done all around the globe.

Try it yourself.

7. Help other people

Let me share a quick insight.

Life is not all about you. I learned this valuable lesson some time back. I was never egoistic, but I always cared for my feelings and my interests.

When I made a shift in my perspective and focused on other people's needs and REALLY try to help them (from the bottom of my heart), I discovered something quite shocking.

Helping others gives me more joy than just fulfilling my own needs.

It changed my whole perspective of life. It changed the way I look at things now.

If you want to help other people, do it authentically. Do not do it just for the sake of it. Show some compassion and empathy. Try putting yourself in their position and see the world from their eyes. Then, do your best to help them.

It will give you more joy than you could ever imagine.

MORNING ROUTINE - START YOUR DAY WITH HAPPINESS AND PRODUCTIVITY

Recently, someone asked me about my habit of waking up early every day and asked me why I do that.

Benefits of waking up early

Disclaimer: if you are a night owl, and that works for you, that's great. There's no need to change, especially if you're happy with it.

But for me, I experienced a huge bump in the quality of my life since joining the 5 AM club. It has helped me in so many ways that I'd never go back. Here are just a few:

1. More gratitude

I love being able to get up and greet a wonderful new day. I suggest creating a morning ritual that includes saying thanks for your blessings. There is a great quote by the Dalai Lama, "Every day, think as you wake up, 'today I am fortunate to have woken up, I am alive, I have a precious human life, I am not going to waste it. I am going to use all my entire energy to develop myself, to expand my heart out to others, to achieve enlightenment for the benefit of all beings, I am going to have kind thoughts towards others, I am not going to get angry or think badly about others, I am going to benefit others as much as I can.' "

2. Head start on rest on the world

I used to start my day by jumping out of bed, late as usual, and rushing to get myself ready and not get late for work. I would walk into the office looking ruffled and barely awake, irritated, and behind everyone else. Not a great start to the day.

Now, I have a refreshing morning ritual. I've gotten so much done before 8 am. I am early at work, and by the time everyone else gets into work, I've already gotten a head start. There is no better way to start off your day than to wake up early.

3. Quiet time

No yelling, no crying, no soccer balls, no cars, no television noise. The early morning hours are so peaceful. It's my favorite time of day. I truly enjoy that time of peace, that time to myself, when I can think, read, and breathe.

4. Exercise

While we can exercise at any time during the day, I've found that exercising right after work is liable to be canceled because of other things that come up. Morning exercise is virtually never canceled.

5. Productivity

Mornings are the most productive time of day. I like to do some creative work in the morning when there are no distractions before I check my email messages. I get so much more done by starting on my work in the morning. Then, when the evening rolls around, I have no work that I need to do, and I can spend it with my family.

6. Goal time

The sun begins to come up, and the first rays of light begin to shine upon this fresh day.

What do you do with this time?

The most important thing.

If you have a project to complete (let's say you want to write a book), this is the time to form a habit that will make that project happen. A morning writing habit will get the book done. Simply waiting for the perfect moment to start writing will not make it happen.

If something is important, you can make a morning habit of it:

If you want to get fit, create a morning walk habit. Or morning strength training. Or a healthy breakfast with fruits and veggies.

If you want to start a new business, work on it every morning.

If you want to become more mindful during your day, create a morning meditation habit.

If you want to improve your relationship with your spouse, a daily habit of having a pleasant conversation over coffee is a great start.

If you want to journal, make it a morning habit.

Why do I believe the morning is the best time for important habits? I've found the time to be peaceful, quiet, and free from distractions. Some people will work better in the late nights, but I'm usually tired by then. So figure out what is your magic time — I think for most people that will be mornings, but not all.

There are some great habits you can create in the afternoons and evenings too, but I recommend creating a morning routine if you have something important you want to get done.

Make it a routine, and do it in the morning.

A simple but powerful morning routine

As your day begins, it's easy to get lost in the habit of checking emails, social media messages, and the news.

It's incredibly easy to waste your first few hours doing several small, harmless activities ... but the really important stuff gets put off.

The solution, I've found, is to make the first hour of your day the most powerful hour. Treat that first hour as sacred. Do not waste it on trivial things. It should be filled with only the most essential, most life-changing actions.

Essential actions might include:

* Meditating

* Exercising

* Journaling

* Reading

* Writing (or creating in some other way)

* Studying

* Yoga

* Working on your most important task of the day

When I'm able to take those kinds of essential actions in the morning, my whole day is transformed. I am more productive, focused, and optimistic.

Treating this first hour as the most important helps me realize that time is precious. It makes me realize that I have a limited time on my hands and that I have to live every hour with a deep appreciation for it.

My Current Morning Routine

My morning routine has been changed many times over the years. It never stays the same, sometimes changing on a monthly basis. But when things start turning chaotic, I re-center myself and create a morning routine that is helpful for my current situation.

Here's my current morning routine:

- A morning walk (45-minutes)
- Meditation (15 minutes)
- Gratitude Prayer (5 minutes)
- Write down my goals (5 minutes)

Start working on the most important task of the day

When you start a morning routine, keep each action fairly short. I've found it's useful to start small when you first begin. This way, it's easier to form the habit.

Creating Your Powerful Morning Routine

You don't have to choose a combination like me, of course. The idea is to figure out what you need the most in your current life situation and put those activities in your morning routine.

You might not know which combination would work for you … pick something and try it. A good mix might include:

- Some kind of self-reflection activity (meditation, gratitude, journal, etc.)
- Your most important task.
- Something that demands full concentration (any creative work, reading, studying, etc.)
- A physical activity (walking, cycling, yoga, cardio, tai chi, etc.)

You can choose anything that suits you. If you can't concentrate in the morning, maybe take a walk. If you don't like physical activity, maybe relaxing activities like reading, journaling would work great.

The main question to ask yourself is: if you were given an extra hour in the morning, what would you spend it on? What would make the biggest difference in your day?

Then try it. Try the routine for a week or two and see what happens. Modify as needed.

Your day is pretty much formed by how you spend your first hour. If you win the morning, you win the day.

MOTIVATION - 6 TIPS FOR IMPROVED SELF-MOTIVATION

Have you ever found yourself NOT doing the work that you KNOW you should do?

Did you ever set a goal of losing a few pounds till the end of the current month by following a diet & exercise plan but got distracted halfway and couldn't lose the weight on time?

Have you ever slacked off in the middle of a work project and couldn't finish it before the deadline?

Me too.

Motivation is a powerful yet tricky beast.

It is critical for achieving success in any endeavor of life. Now, we are going to dive deeper and look at some of the relatively unknown facts about motivation.

Fact #1 - Motivation is an emotion

Motivation is a special kind of emotion. It's an emotional drive or desire to do something. It pushes us to take action and move towards a specific outcome. Because of this, motivation is crucial for the attainment of any worthwhile goal.

While healthy levels of motivation pump you up to take action, lack of the same can make you lazy and stagnant.

The more motivated you are, the more compelling taking action becomes. The lesser your motivation level, the more you are likely to procrastinate and make excuses. You can call motivation the archrival of procrastination and laziness.

Fact #2 - A blessing in disguise

Motivation is a blessing. If you are motivated to do something great, consider yourself 'blessed.'

Very few people are blessed with the motivation to make things better. If you have the compulsion to create a better future for yourself and society, you are extremely fortunate. Don't take your motivation lightly. You are one in a thousand individuals who have the desire to change.

Do yourself and your society a favor and capitalize on it. It will not be there forever.

HOW TO INCREASE YOUR MOTIVATION?

Now we come to the core of this chapter - how to increase motivation and sustain it at high levels. The techniques for increasing motivation mentioned below are among the most effective ones that I have found after trying out everything under the sun for more than 13 long years.

I have tried them all - from NLP and punishment/reward to visualization and energy works such as EFT, and these are some of the best ones I ever came across.

1. Find your "why"

The first very effective method is to make a list of WHY you want to achieve your goals. What are the reasons for which you crave your desire? How will the realization of your goals help you and others? What will it allow you to do or feel? What positive changes will it bring?

These are the reasons for which you want to acquire your goals.

And your reasons can be of any kind - financial, physical, spiritual, or mental. Whatever they may be, if they make you 'feel' even slightly motivated, add them to your list. Make sure your reasons are authentic, which means they are your personal reasons. Whenever you think about them, you feel excited.

The higher the number of reasons in your list, the better it is.

Once you have prepared your list, review it at least three times a day. More than any individual reason, it's the cumulative impact of this list that will boost your motivation to a much higher level. And best of all, it is available to you all the time. You can view this list at any moment you need.

Now some people ask why this has to be a 'written' list. Why can't they just have these in mind?

The answer is: writing down these reasons is very powerful. There has been a lot of research done about the positive impact of the written word. Whenever we write something down, it affects our subconscious mind at a very deep level. Additionally, you can view this list anytime you need a boost in your motivation.

Another important point is to make sure your reasons are positive, not negative. For example, "I will be fully financially independent when I achieve my goal" is a positive reason. Don't write it as "I will be able to pay my bills and move out of this horrible situation."

See? The first reason is written in a positive tone and feels much more uplifting and powerful. The second makes you focus on the negative, even if its overall meaning is positive.

"Life is about focusing on what you want, not on what you don't want" - **Anthony Robbins.**

So make sure your reasons are written in a positive tone, which will make you focus on the positive benefits of achieving your goals.

To recap:

• Make a list of positive, empowering reasons for you to achieve your goals. Make sure you select reasons which make you FEEL pumped up.

• Write it down on a piece of paper.

• Review this "why" list at least three times in a day, preferably once in the morning after waking up and two more times later in the day.

2. Cut-off all distractions

Distractions kill motivation.

Here is what you do if you want to achieve your goals and get ahead in life...

Completely cut out everything that doesn't support you.

Don't eat any type of food that doesn't support you.

Don't look at any type of influence like television or media or celebrity gossip websites.

Do not play video games.

Do not watch movies.

Minimize alcohol consumption.

Minimize interactions with people who distract you from moving towards your goals.

Do not do anything that makes you waste your time.

When you set a goal, you make a commitment - it must be the single focus of your day-to-day life.

If you want to be relaxed, have fun, and goof around, don't set a goal.

Setting a goal demands your complete attention, and if you are unwilling to give up all other leisure activities, do not set a goal.

Because there is no middle ground. Either you are fully committed to a single objective or not. If you mix both - committing to a goal AND being relaxed - it is a recipe for disaster.

You will neither be relaxed nor motivated. You will be confused and worried all the time about what you should do and shouldn't do.

Decide what you want to do. If you want to relax and take things easy, do that. If you want to achieve something important to you, commit fully to it and cut-off all distractions.

If you choose to follow the latter, you will experience an unbelievable surge in your motivation levels.

3. Set small, manageable goals

If you have a big task to accomplish, and it feels daunting... it is better to break it down into a series of smaller steps.

For example, suppose you have a goal of getting into shape. It can be very vague and confusing by itself. In this case, you have to break it down into smaller, more manageable goals.

Goal #1 - Take a gym membership.

Goal #2 - Ask a professional what exercises you should do.

Goal #3 - Find out your daily protein requirement.

Goal #4 - Add greens like kale, spinach, broccoli & clean meats like chicken to your diet.

Goal #5 - Start drinking 2-3 liters of water each day.

Goal #6 - etc...

In this example, "getting into shape" is a pretty broad and vague term in itself. It does not convey what exactly needs to be done. By breaking it into a series of smaller goals will allow you to know exactly what you have to do and when. It gives clarity to the whole process and increases the odds of you taking action massively.

So, break down all your big goals into a series of smaller goals. It *really* helps!

4. Momentum is the key

Momentum, also called forward momentum, is the "flow" you have when you are taking action consistently. It's like if you are already going to the gym 5 days a week, it will not be difficult to work out 6 days a week. Because you are already taking action, you have forward momentum.

That is why starting a new project is so hard. It takes a lot more effort to initiate something. But once it picks up the momentum, it becomes easier to maintain.

It's much easier to keep a ball rolling than to get it moving from a standstill.

It works amazing for increasing your motivation. If you are just starting out, do small tasks which demand little effort from you. For example, if you want to lose weight, start drinking green tea every morning instead of coffee and be persistent with that. After a few days, add 30 minutes of walk in your day. Soon after that, replace oily and fried food with green vegetables.

Take it easy in the beginning. Start small and do activities that require only a little effort. Once you get comfortable, begin taking up challenges which demand more. For example - eat only healthy food, cut off all sugar and processed food, exercise regularly, strictly following your schedule, etc.

As you complete smaller challenges, you will start gaining momentum. It will become increasingly easier to take action regularly.

As you keep challenging yourself with more and more tasks, your momentum will get stronger. The more momentum you gain, the easier it will be to take action regularly. Soon, you will reach a point where it will be easier to take more action than to stop.

This is the power of forward momentum.

It will have a spill-over effect on other areas of your life. Momentum is energy, and by practicing it, you are putting energy into your everyday life. You will feel more alive and vibrant. The joy of taking down challenges, coupled with satisfaction from moving in the direction of your desires will create such joy, you will not want to stop.

At this point, the power of momentum is on your side. You will breeze past any obstacles & problems without giving a second thought. It's like shifting to the fast lane to success. Moving forward will become your default way of thinking and behaving.

But you must know one more fact about momentum. Just as the momentum is gained by taking action, it can decrease or even completely die out if you stop taking action. You'll have to take action consistently to build and maintain high levels of momentum.

And the more momentum you build, the easier it will be to take more action, which creates more momentum. It is a powerful, upward-spinning cycle.

If you stop taking action, your momentum will start decreasing. And with enough stall time, it will fade away completely.

Keep both of these factors in mind -

a) Taking regular action creates and sustains momentum.

b) The more momentum you build, the easier it gets to take more action.

c) Being stagnant will kill momentum.

Use this insight to your advantage and never lose your momentum. The higher your momentum, the stronger your motivation would be.

5. Deliberate exposure

Another extremely effective way to increase your motivation level is "deliberate exposure."

Whenever you have some free time, immerse yourself in pictures, audio & information of your goal(s). Read books, listen to audio, view pictures, read information about your chief objective.

For example, if your goal is to buy a brand new Volkswagen Jetta, read its reviews, go to its website, read glowing ownership experiences, watch long-ride videos on YouTube, read about its earlier models and technical advancements.

As we go through our day, there are lots of things which demand our attention like work, family responsibilities, hobbies, friends, etc.

Going through our daily grind, we tend to forget about our goals.

The human mind tends to put things in the background if it's not something that demands immediate attention. And because goals usually require a period of time to accomplish, it tends to get 'out of focus' for the majority of the day. This causes a big loss in the intensity of motivation.

Let's suppose you reviewed goals this morning and are feeling pumped up. You feel very motivated and are raring to go. But later during the day, you get caught up in some other work-related issue, or maybe a friend needs your urgent help.

It's very common to forget about your goal when you get caught up in the daily chores. It causes a loss of motivation, and worse, you start to get thoughts like - "oh, I cannot focus on my goals for long. Maybe I am just not cut out for this kind of thing," or "I keep forgetting about my goals, maybe they are not so important for me?"

It takes a toll on your feelings of desire. Slowly but surely, your motivation starts going down.

The solution here is to deliberately expose yourself to your goal so you can see it, hear it, and read about it. It will make sure your goals are in your mind all the time.

Whenever you have some "free" time, instead of watching random music videos, watch something related to your goal - any new information, review, people's opinions, how other successful people achieved it, and so on.

It can be videos, books, songs, blogs, audiobooks, pictures, or anything else related to your goal. I call it - "deliberate exposure."

Dwelling on your desire.

Immersing yourself in it.

But to clear things up, it does not mean that you should watch videos all day and not take action. Deliberate exposure is meant to be done in spare time, in place of other unneeded activities we do when we get free.

For example, you want to grow your business and have scheduled marketing work from 11 am to 4 pm, do not waste those precious five hours by reading an article about the luxurious lifestyle of big business owners.

When it's time to work, do your best work. When you get some free time to do other activities, you can choose to spend it reading/watching anything related to your main objective.

It's your answer against distractions and negative influences. That's another positive aspect of 'Deliberate exposure.' It protects you from indulging in some activity that may cause you to be distracted for the whole day. It guards your mind against other negative influences like gossiping, reading rumors, wasting time on social media because you are spending your free time focusing on your goal.

As you can imagine, deliberate exposure can boost your concentration, productivity, and motivation to a much higher level than before. In my own experience, it makes the mind completely focused on the goal. Later, regardless of the activity I'd be doing, my goals were always on my mind. I found it very effective. It truly made my mental focus stick to my desires all the time. The surge in my levels of motivation was amazing.

To recap:

1. When you are working, put your complete attention into doing the best work possible.

2. In your free time, you should be doing the following:

- Watch videos, movies, TV programs related to your goals.

- Listen to songs, audiobooks, and podcasts on your chosen objective.
- Read books, articles, news, and blogs to collect new information on your goals.
- Talk about it with open-minded people who support you and your cause.
- Create a vision board - a place where you keep different pictures of your goals.

Many people set a goal for themselves but do not focus on it frequently. Deliberate exposure will keep your goal at the forefront of your mind and ensure that the intensity of desire never fades.

6. Have faith

(If you are an atheist, you can replace the word "god" with the universe, source energy, greater good, etc.)

Fear kills more dreams than failure ever will.

Fear kills motivation.

One of the core pillars of strength against fear is faith. Have strong faith in yourself, your vision, and god. A strong, unshakable faith can move mountains, and a weak one can stop you from taking even the first step.

Realize that every man on earth is created equal. The richest and the most successful people have the same physical brain and body structure as you have. Nobody is cut from a different cloth.

We all are more similar than we are different. The basic foundation is similar for everyone. It's the way you use what you have been given that makes all the difference.

Successful people use their time & resources on things like reading, training, taking action, finding solutions, making progress, etc.

Using what you have to its full potential is what separates the best from the rest.

Believe in yourself and your vision. Right now, at this very moment, you have all the resources to become the most successful, happy, healthy person in the world. You are more than enough at this very moment.

Do not doubt yourself.

Think BIG!

Go for your goals!

Have UNSHAKABLE faith!

Most of the time, success is all about how strong your faith is, the conviction with which you believe in yourself. Your faith, at any point, should never be anything less than unbreakable.

There are two reasons for it -

1) Nobody is cut from a different cloth. You have similar resources to the ultra-successful people.

2) A breakable faith is of no use at all.

The bigger your goal, the stronger your faith needs to be. Bigger goals need more time and effort. They also contain harder challenges. In such cases, having an unshakable faith is necessary because it will be tested many times over!

"None of us know what might happen even the next minute, yet still we go forward. Because we trust. Because we have faith." -**Paulo Coelho.**

When all else fails, you can come back to your faith to take shelter from chaos & uncertainty. It's like an oasis in the vast desert. It is your place of certainty and calm. Strong faith has the power to keep you going even when it seems like all doors are closed.

Your faith keeps you going.

Faith and fear cannot co-exist together. They cancel each other out. In your heart, there is a place for only one - faith or fear. You get to decide which one should exist. You are the creator of both. You have complete power over their existence.

Many people don't realize they have such power. Realize this truth and use it in your favor.

"Faith and fear both have you believing in something which you cannot see... You decide." -**Bob Proctor.**

Always have complete faith in yourself, your vision, and your goal. A lack of faith will weaken your resolve when facing difficulty and setbacks, while an unshakable faith will drive you towards the life of your dreams.

Believe in **yourself** and all that you **are**. Know that there is something inside you that is **greater** than any obstacle.

Believe you can and **you are halfway there**.

Positive Energy Principle #4

CONFIDENCE - 8 HACKS TO BOOST YOUR SELF-CONFIDENCE

Self-confidence is a superpower. It is the foundation of all great success and achievement. Once you start believing in yourself, things start happening.

Self-confidence plays a big role in achieving any goal in life, yet so many people struggle with it.

"Low self-confidence is like driving through life with your hand brake on." - Maxwell Maltz.

People with high self-confidence generally like themselves and are willing to take risks to achieve their personal and professional goals. They also think positively about the future.

A person who lacks self-confidence has difficulty believing they can achieve their goals, has a low expectation of what they deserve in life.

The good news is that self-confidence is something you can improve!

But to improve self-confidence, we need to find out what it really is.

What is self-confidence?

Self-confidence is the value you have in your mind. It does not matter what everyone else thinks about you. What's important is what you think about yourself.

Your self-confidence determines your self-respect, your happiness, the amount of love you give to yourself and others, how you take care of yourself, how resilient you are, and your overall level of success in life.

Self-confidence makes life worth living. It affects EVERYTHING! Your success, relationships, health, perspectives, peace, and the amount of happiness you allow yourself to feel and your reactions to the various events happening in your life.

Benefits of high self-confidence

Highly confident people experience the following:

1. More joy & happiness

2. More enthusiasm

3. High energy levels

4. More authenticity

5. Less social anxiety

6. Desire to achieve more

7. More compassion towards self and others

8. Increased focus and concentration

9. Ease in social situations

10. Non-judgmental towards self and others

11. Less fear and worry

There are many other benefits aside from those mentioned above. The point is, self-confidence increases your quality of life more than anything else.

Effects of low self-confidence

1. People having low self-confidence feel a sense of lack. An internal voice is telling them that they are not enough.

2. They feel bored and lack energy. They are less likely to take good care of themselves and others. They are less likely to go to the gym, eat healthy food, and groom themselves properly.

3. The willingness to achieve success goes away. They feel a huge surge of internal resistance when they think about taking action towards their goals.

4. Low self-confidence people procrastinate a lot. They self-sabotage themselves.

5. Criticism from others has a big emotional impact on them, and the whole thing keeps repeating in their mind all day.

6. People with low self-confidence compare themselves with other people and always end up feeling inferior.

7. Even if someone or something puts them in a fun mood for the moment, Low self-confidence people return to their negative, bored mood as soon as that fun runs out. They leech positive emotions from other people, which drive others away.

8. Lousy relationship with other people. Low self-confidence hinders their ability to fully love and care about other people.

9. Lesser emotional stability. A person with low self-confidence is likely to be angry, upset, enraged, cry, depressed easily than a person having high self-confidence.

10. Low self-confidence causes a negative spiral. A person already feeling down, does things like arguing with other people, procrastinate, eat a lot, does not take care of himself, etc. These things make him feel worse, and his confidence gets even lower. This is the negative, downward spiral created by low self-confidence.

Obviously, we want to have high self-confidence. How can we get it? And if we have low self-confidence, how do we increase it?

8 hacks to boost your self-confidence

1. Take action on your core values

This is the single BIGGEST factor that determines your self-confidence. You have some core values, which are nothing but your ideals, goals, dreams, rules, aspirations, etc. To raise and maintain high self-confidence, it is critically important that you TAKE ACTION and MOVE TOWARDS your core values.

Yes, I said to take action. You have to take action. High self-confidence is the result of taking action towards your values.

Your actions create confidence.

Furthermore, you have to take action daily. The ups and downs of self-confidence happen on a daily basis. It is crazy to think about, but on a day when I don't take any action and move closer to my values, I feel my confidence drop rapidly!

On the other hand, on the days when I do take action, my confidence soars high as well.

I strongly suggest that you get crystal clear about what your core values are and then take action on a daily basis. It's all about personal integrity that comes from knowing that you are not lying to yourself by watching TV when you should be working on your pending project.

Taking action towards your values raises your integrity, which in turn raises your self-confidence.

This particular concept made the single BIGGEST impact on my confidence among all techniques mentioned in this chapter. Even if you do nothing else, just adopt this concept. You will be surprised by how effective it is.

2. Plan ahead

"One important key to success is self-confidence. An important key to self-confidence is preparation." — Arthur Ashe.

When you are prepared, you're more confident to take action.

Planning is deciding in advance what is to be done, when & where it is to be done, how it is to be done, and by whom.

It's a road map of activities to be done, so you move towards your objective.

This single idea - planning - is the reason your dreams become your reality. It converts an idea in your mind to something real... something which can be done in the present moment to ACTUALLY move towards your desired outcome.

For example, Joe gets the idea that he should start his own business. He likes the thought of being an entrepreneur and feels excited. He thinks he would certainly start working on his business... soon.

He keeps this thought in his mind and gets caught up in his daily routine and responsibilities. The thought and the excitement of being an entrepreneur soon start fading away. And whenever the thoughts of starting his own business come to his mind, he justifies, "oh, but I don't have enough time. I will do it later."

And that time never comes...

I have seen countless times people get an insight, an idea about what they should do, and they let that idea fade away. It's very disheartening. I have been in this place myself many times, so I know exactly how it feels.

But let's take another example, this time, Joe gets it right. He does not let the idea fade away.

First, he writes down the thought on a piece of paper (or a mobile notepad). When he gets home after work, he opens a diary and writes down that idea on top of the page.

Then he starts thinking about every possible activity or person who could help him move in the direction of his goals... Read "how to start a business" books, attend seminars on building a business, get his friend's entrepreneur contact to advise on what he should do to create his product, and so on.

(Bonus tip: nobody at the start of their journey knew EXACTLY how they would reach their goals, and this is not important at first. The most important thing at the beginning is to DECIDE what is it that you want and trust that you will reach your goals.)

Joe makes a list of these and starts doing them one by one regularly. Each one of these activities moves Joe one step closer to his goal. Every activity leads to new insights, and soon he gets a clear vision of the path that he has to take. He breaks down the whole process into a series of small, actionable steps. Eventually, Joe starts his business on a small scale, and its expansion becomes his new goal.

With time and persistence, Joe will eventually succeed.

Joe was able to start his business because he did not let the thought fade away by doing something about it. He wrote down his goal on paper. He thought about activities and people that could help. He made a list.

This is called planning. It does not have to be very thorough and scientifically precise. Any simple plan would do. As you gain experience by working on it, you would make changes in your plan to make it better and better.

Plan ahead. It's a great way to boost your self-confidence.

3. Practice the skill!

One of the best ways to feel more confident is to be more competent. Become better at what you do. Improve your craft. Some people think they can become more confident just by affirming positive thoughts.

Not always.

Sometimes, you lack confidence because you are bad at something that you do. For example, if you are learning to play guitar and people ask you to play a song in front of a crowd, you will feel nervous and anxious.

No amount of positive affirmations would help here. You are not good at playing guitar, and now have to play a song in front of the entire crowd. Obliviously, you would be nervous and anxious.

The only way to acquire high self-confidence in a situation like this is to become good at playing guitar.

You need to practice, practice, and practice to become good at what you do. This will boost your self-confidence.

It will also have a spill-over effect on other areas of your life. For example, you have mastered the skill of real estate sales and are earning great amounts of income.

The confidence boost you get from being financially well-off will show up when you talk to people. It would increase your social confidence as well. When people talk to you, they will feel your confidence. This is the "spill-over effect" of developing self-confidence.

So practice and become better at what you do. Become more competent, and confidence will soon follow.

4. Go outside your comfort zone

Our mind wants comfort and is afraid of discomfort and change. We are well aware of the thoughts and feelings that reside in our comfort zone. We know the kind of life that exists there.

Anytime we try to push beyond that comfort zone, the mind tries desperately to get back into the familiar territory. At any cost, including our long-term health, success, and happiness.

Among all the skills I've learned in the past 13 years to change my life, one skill stands out:

Stepping outside the comfort zone

If you become good at it, you can master pretty much anything. You can beat procrastination, get more done, become more fit, eat healthier, earn more money, learn a new language, explore new cultures, speak on a stage, surpass your fears, and reach your true potential.

The comfort zone is a bubble. It feels comfortable but also boring because it prevents growth and change. Leaving our comfort zone gives us a better understanding of who we are and what we like when we expose ourselves to new experiences.

However, stepping outside of your comfort zone is uncomfortable and scary. We all have a comfort zone where we feel at ease and in control. But every now and then, you need to step outside and be challenged. Be frightened. Be stimulated. It makes you feel alive and excited about the progress.

The whole idea of stepping out of your comfort zone is uncomfortable. Pick something that scares you each day, then go ahead and do it.

Each time you do what scares you, your comfort zone expands. Even if you take a tiny step forward, it's still progress. You tried. You pushed through. You survived to tell the tale. Now try again.

When you familiarize yourself with the things that scare you, you will find it easy to step out of your comfort zone when the need arises. It will become normal to do what used to scare you earlier!

A powerful technique to get out of your comfort zone

Progressive Desensitization

Progressive desensitization, also known as graduated exposure therapy, is a type of behavior therapy developed by South African psychiatrist Joseph Wolpe. It is used in the field of clinical psychology to help many people effectively overcome phobias and other anxiety disorders that are based on classical conditioning.

The main idea of Progressive desensitization is to expose yourself to the situation you are scared of and slowly increase in intensity and duration of exposure.

Here are the exact steps:

Step 1: In this technique, a person in therapy is asked to "mentally" confront the fear or situation by picturing it in one's mind. For example, a woman with the fear of flying might imagine sitting on a flight.

Step 2: Once she becomes comfortable with the mental pictures of her sitting on a plane, she is exposed to real-life objects and scenarios. For example, she might go to the airport and watch a plane take off.

Step 3: Once she becomes comfortable watching planes taking off, she steps inside the plane for a moment and then comes back to the airport.

Step 4: Once she is comfortable going inside the plane, she takes a short flight to a nearby city.

Step 5: The next step for her to take longer flights and become comfortable with them.

This technique is used to treat a variety of phobias, ranging from mild social anxiety to crippling fear of snakes. You can use it to step outside your comfort zone. Remember to take small steps forward and become comfortable with every step before moving to the next one.

(Disclaimer: if you have an intense phobia or anxiety, seek professional help. Please do not do it on your own.)

5. Stop comparing yourself with others

People with low self-confidence tend to compare themselves with other people. And usually, they end up feeling worse about themselves. This is because we only evaluate other people's apparent strengths we initially see... their looks, their money, their status, etc.

We have no idea about their weaknesses.

While we don't fully know them, we are completely aware of OUR weaknesses. We compare our weaknesses against their PERCEIVED strengths... and we end up short.

This whole comparison thing is complete nonsense. Our view is distorted. A person is never static. We are always changing...

growing mentally, emotionally, financially, physically, spiritually. We have a vast number of unique traits. For example – our unique outlook, life experience, beliefs, body type, perspectives, likes and dislikes, how we can cook, how we love, how we write, what we dream, the way we live, our past, our friends, our family, our choices, and it goes on and on....

When we are made up of THOUSANDS of UNIQUE traits, and we are CONSTANTLY CHANGING and growing every moment... how can we determine our self-worth by comparing one aspect of ourselves with the other person? Is it even possible? NO.

Remember, we are all unique. Our creator made every one of us special, and we were sent here for a purpose. That purpose is unique to each individual. So stop comparing yourself with others because it is not possible. Instead, accept yourself completely, then find your purpose, your mission, and work on it with all your heart.

You will be filled with a sense of integrity and high self-confidence.

6. Take care of yourself

"Beauty is self-confidence applied directly to the face!"

Another way to raise your self-confidence is to take proper care of your health and grooming. Go to the gym. Wear well-fitted clothes which look good on you. Eat healthy food which nourishes your body. Avoid junk foods. Get a better haircut. Take care of your skin and hair. Invest in yourself... both money and time.

When you are working hard in the gym or going the extra mile to shop for healthy food, your mind will realize that you value yourself. Your self-confidence will soar. The added effect will be that you feel much healthier and attractive because you have been taking care of yourself. On top of that, you will feel amazing because you took the pains to take care of yourself. Your mind will think, "I really value myself."

When you are in this kind of state, you will have no shortage of self-confidence.

7. Look for the good in other people

There is a lovely story about a boy who had a fight with his mom and went to a top of a mountain and shouted in the valley – "mom, I hate u….. I hate you…. I hate you…"

An echo returned from the valley – "I hate you… I hate you… I hate you…" The boy was startled. He ran back to his house and told his mom that there was a mean little boy in the valley that shouted at him – I hate you.

Mom smiled. She took her boy to that spot again and told him to shout again, but this time he has to shout – "I love you… I love you… I love you…" Boy did as she said.

To his surprise, now there was a sweet little boy in the valley shouting – "I love you… I love you… I love you…" His mom told him that when you love other people, they love you back.

The world works exactly like this. What you give out, you receive back 100 folds. If you give out love and care to others, you will get affection and support back. If you give out anger and hatred, you will receive the same in return.

It is really important to treat others well. When you treat others well, you feel good. And when they treat you well in return, you feel good. It's a win-win situation.

But how exactly will you start treating others well?

How you look at other people determines how you will treat them. For example, if you see others as basically good people, it is much more likely that you will treat them with warmth. On the other hand, if you see other people as self-centered, your behavior will be cold and standoffish towards them.

So always, always remember this golden rule of life:

Always ask yourself – what is good in this person? How can I find his/her good qualities?

When you ask this question, your mind will zoom in on the other person's positive qualities, and you will look at them with admiration and warmth. Others will feel that and treat you similarly.

Man is a social creature. Our ability to form a community is our biggest strength. It is in our genes. When you treat others well and connect with them, your self-confidence and personal integrity rise because you are living the way you were designed by nature.

Try treating others exceptionally well for a week. See how better you feel.

8. Run positive mental movies

Positive mental movie is a technique where you imagine yourself going through a difficult situation and coming out victorious.

It's a very effective technique for changing your beliefs and improving self-confidence.

Medical science has proved that the human mind cannot differentiate between something vividly imagined and real life.

In an experiment, researchers placed scanners on an athlete's body and got him to imagine running on a track in as much detail as possible. Scanners revealed that during the imagination, his muscles were activating in the same manner as when doing the actual physical activity of running on a track.

Since then, multiple researchers have verified the positive effect of running mental movies on the actual performance of an individual. Now, this fact is widely accepted in sports psychology, and trainers put a huge emphasis on regular mental practice along with physical ones.

This is a very powerful concept, and its possibilities are virtually unlimited. For example, suppose you have social anxiety. You feel nervous about going to a party and talking to people you don't know. If you visualize for 10 - 15 minutes that you're in a party full of strangers and are feeling relaxed & calm while socializing with them, your mind will soon accept it as truth, and your social anxiety would decrease by a good amount.

I used visualization to get rid of my fear of public speaking. In the past, I had some pretty bad experiences with public speaking. I used to stutter my words, lose my train of thought, wondering what people are thinking about me while standing on stage. It was pretty embarrassing.

But when I found out about this technique and how it works, I decided to give it a try. So, on the night before my big presentation, I closed my eyes and ran a mental movie about giving a speech in a room full of people.

I felt the same anxiety as when I stand on stage in real life. It was pretty much the same feeling. But, I forced myself to deliver my speech as best as I could. As this was in my imagination, whenever I messed up, I stopped & repeat it again and try to do it correctly this time.

It took 15 tries for me to lose almost all of my anxiety while delivering my speech.

The next day, when I actually got on stage, it felt quite familiar. As if I had done it before. I did feel 'some' anxiety, but it was quite manageable. My speech went quite well, and people came up to me afterward to tell me how clear I was with my message.

Since that day, I became a firm believer in the power of positive mental movies. I used it again in many other areas, and it always helped.

It is a very powerful technique when done correctly. Follow this simple, step-by-step method.

How to run positive mental movies?

1. First, sit or lie down in a relaxed, quiet environment. Make sure there are no distractions like excessive noise or lights. You

should feel relaxed in this environment. For most people, such a place would be their bedroom.

2. Close your eyes. Take a few deep, relaxed breaths. Consciously relax your body and mind.

3. Once you are feeling relaxed, close your eyes. Start imagining that you have reached your goal. You have achieved what you wanted and now are filled with excitement & joy. Imagine it in as much detail as possible. It should be easy because it's something you really want. You will start feeling really good.

Note: Don't worry. You don't have to do it perfectly. Just add as many details as you can. After little practice, you will be able to run the scenes in much more detail.

4. Now, keep viewing that vision (and feeling good) for few moments (1 to 5 minutes).

5. Open your eyes and relax.

That's it. It is a very simple process (quite relaxing too), but its effects are AMAZINGLY powerful. I wholeheartedly recommend this technique to improve your self-confidence and condition your mind for success.

Now it's your turn.

All of the techniques mentioned in this chapter are simple and can be done by anyone who's willing, and the return of benefits is much greater than the time & effort invested.

Every day is a new beginning. Take a deep breath, smile, and try again. Don't ever let anything dull your sparkle.

Positive Energy Principle #5

Happiness - 4 Simple Ways to Find Happiness and Peace

We wonder, "I wish I could be happier." The idea of a life full of joy and fulfillment may seem far-fetched to some; it is definitely possible. There are people living their lives blissfully. Every day they feel pleasant, joyful, and upbeat. These individuals are doing something different than the rest of us. They follow timeless principles for happiness which have been passed down generation after generation.

In this section, we will look at these principles and how to apply them in our life.

Who runs the show?

We are creatures of habit. Most of the thoughts that come up in our minds are automatic. They are habitual. Studies show 85% of the thoughts we have today are repeats from yesterday.

Most of these thoughts are from the subconscious part of our brain. They are below our awareness but when they arise, we *feel* their effect.

Have you ever had this experience - you were completely focused on your work but started feeling bad all of a sudden. Later, when you stopped the work and paid attention, you found that you are upset over an event that happened yesterday or this early morning?

This is our sub-conscious at play.

It is a part of our brain that records memories and feelings that are attached to those memories. When you think about the time when you got your first paycheck, how do you feel?

The good news is, we can influence our subconscious mind by changing our perception and thought process.

Let's look at the thought processes of some of the most influential and happiest people in the world and how they perceive their environment that makes them so peaceful & optimistic.

Desire: the creator of pain and pleasure

Desires give birth to pleasure. It thrills you. But as soon as a new desire is born, it also gives birth to the sensation of its *lack* in your present life situation. That's a pain.

If someone asks me, "what is the greatest obstacle in our search for happiness?" I would say - the concept of desire.

We are obsessed with desire. We think all desires much be fulfilled for us to be happy. We see nothing beyond desire.

On the other hand, "spiritual" people of our society preach the importance of letting go of all desires. They say, "letting go of all desire is the ideal and supreme way of being."

But when we look closely, neither people obsessed with desire nor spiritual people advocating lack of desire seem to be truly happy.

What's going on here?

To get an answer, we have to go deeper.

The whole world revolves around desire. There is not a single living person on this earth that is completely free of desire. Desire brings meaning to our life. Without any desire, we would be dead inside.

Imagine you meet a person who lost all desire, has no meaning in life, and is going to commit suicide. You instill a desire inside that person, and he suddenly wants to live. He has a reason to live. He now has a purpose.

That is the power of desire. Nobody is completely free from desire, and neither should you strive for the desire-less state.

Spiritual people, who advocate letting go of desires, don't realize that their desire to live a desire-free life is also a desire.

It is a trap.

No one can be free of all desire.

So what about happiness? How is desire connected to happiness?

As soon as we form a desire in our mind, it gives birth to feelings of pleasure. We expect ourselves to be happy when we would achieve it.

So is desire happiness itself?

Not really.

Any new desire, along with the promise of happiness, also gives birth to the feeling of lack of whatever we want at the present moment. It causes pain.

If there was no pain, we would be happy just by thinking about our desire. No one would actually strive to attain it.

But the story of pain does not end here.

* If your goal is so big that you doubt you will achieve it, it creates pain.

* If you managed to achieve your goal, the feelings of pleasure would last only for a few days. Afterward, the emptiness and need for even more pleasure would consume your attention again. It is painful.

After going through all aspects of desire, we can say that desire is the creator of both pleasure and pain, and in the long run, the pain created by desire outweighs the pleasure we get.

So is there a way to achieve the happiness that is free of pain and pleasure?

Is it possible to attain pure, lasting happiness?

The real happiness

The true form of happiness is peace. It is the only state of mind that is free from both pain and pleasure. Not only is it free from them, but it is also far superior to either of them.

Peace is the state where you expect nothing and accept everything. You are unaffected by the presence or absence of any shiny object. You are peaceful at this very moment.

Unlike pain and pleasure - which are inseparable from each other - peace does not fade away. You can be peaceful for your entire life. It does not lack anything. It is complete within itself.

It does not need any advice, approval, appreciation, or glory. When a person experiences peace, he experiences contentment with the absence of pain or pleasure.

Pain and pleasure are intertwined. One cannot exist without another. Peace has no such attachments. It stands on its own. A person can live in a state of peace for all eternity. Even if it gets interrupted, you don't have to wait for days or months to get it back. You can instantly go back to feeling peaceful.

Peace is the real, long-lasting happiness. If you want to be happy, do not strive for pleasure or to avoid pain. It will not last. You would end up running in circles around pain and pleasure.

Instead, change the paradigm. Focus on being peaceful. Learn about how to become peaceful in your day-to-day life.

There are some practices that allow you to be in a state of peace. They are simple and can be easily practiced by anyone who is willing. Some of them are:

1. Being in the present moment

2. Being grateful.

3. Letting go of the past.

While it is not a comprehensive list, it's a good way to start exploring the peaceful state of being.

Being in the present moment

How can you bring calm to a stressful, chaotic day?

The answer is: by being in the present moment.

No matter how chaotic your day is, no matter how stressful it is, being in the present moment is like an oasis in the desert. It will change your day, and it's incredibly simple.

When people get asked what prevents them from having a peaceful day, some of the responses we get:

~ Overburdened at work.

~ Cell phone.

~ Social media.

~ News.

~ Kids.

~ Cooking, dishes, laundry.

~ Needless interruptions.

~ Lack of control. Constant "urgent" things at work.

~ My own monkey mind.

How being in the present moment helps?

By looking at all of the problems above, we can see that all the problems are entirely in mind. Sure, some of them seem external, like work, kids, house chores, and digital distractions. But how our mind responds to those external forces is the problem.

If you are present to the moment, the external things are no longer a problem because there is only you at this moment, going through a single task. There are not a million other things you need to worry about at once.

If your kid interrupts you, you stress out because you have so many other things in your mind, and your kid is adding one more to it. It overwhelms you. You freak out.

Instead, you can be present. Now there is only you and the child. You can be fully present with your child and be grateful to have this moment with her.

If you get an urgent task while you were doing some other work, you stress out because you already have a million things to do and not enough time to do them.

Or you can be in the present moment and focus completely on that "urgent" task, and now there is only one task and you. When you're done, you can calmly move on to the next task.

Cell phones, emails, Social media, and other digital distractions don't interrupt you if we put them away and be completely present with the *one current task*.

If we need to call, email, or use social media, we can set aside everything else and just be present with that one digital task.

Being in the present moment is a way to handle any problem, any distraction, any stressor. It allows millions of other things to fade away, leaving you with one task at this moment.

How to practice being in the present moment?

1. Meditation

The best way to become more present in your daily life is to practice meditation. Meditation trains your mind to be in the present moment. But realize that meditation is a daily practice.

You cannot discontinue meditation after six months, thinking now you don't need it.

Mediation works exactly like going to the gym. When you keep doing it, you will feel increasingly more present in the moment in your daily life. When you stop, within a few days, you will feel the difference. You will start to fall back into your old thought pattern.

Nothing is constant. What doesn't grow, starts dying. This applies strongly to meditation. Start doing meditation daily. Its benefits are much greater than the amount of time & effort you exert.

Now the main questions are — How long your daily meditation sessions should be & How to do meditation?

The Answer to the first question is — it depends upon you. I find 15 minutes of daily meditation enough. It makes me more present & calm in my day-to-day life.

Here is a simple, step-by-step guide for doing meditation effectively.

How to Meditate?

a) Set an alarm for 15 minutes.

b) Sit comfortably on a chair, keeping your back relaxed & upright. Use Cushion if you need to.

c) Close your eyes and start noticing your breath coming in and out. Notice everything about it: when it enters your nostrils to when it goes in your diaphragm. The movement of your stomach going up and down, etc.

d) Eventually, your mind will start thinking about something. You will get lost in your thoughts. You lose focus on your breath and start dwelling on the thought itself. It's Ok.

e) Whenever you catch yourself focusing on your thoughts instead of being aware of your breath, gently and calmly shift your focus to your breath.

f) What will certainly happen is you will lose your focus again and get lost in thoughts. Again, simply shift your focus to your breath calmly.

g) Keep doing this for 15 minutes till your alarm rings.

Note: Don't force yourself to keep your mind empty all the time. Your mind will think and that's what we want. Actually, your mind gets stronger when you shift your focus back from your thoughts to your breath. This back-and-forth of awareness is what strengthens your mental muscles. It's like a gym for your mind.

This simple exercise will increase the performance of your mind (i.e., clarity of thoughts, concentration, willpower, focus) to astronomical levels. Its effectiveness is unmatched. Studies all over the world are attesting the positive effect of meditation on our brain. I would even confess that I would not be able to finish this book if it wasn't for meditation.

Another KEY point related to meditation is consistency. It doesn't matter whether you meditate for 5 minutes or an hour; just make sure you are meditating REGULARLY. Because if you miss one day, you would probably find an excuse to miss the next day. Be consistent. Don't skip a day. If you are extremely busy, meditate for 5 minutes just before you sleep at night. Make it a regular habit.

It will not take long before you start noticing the positive effects of meditation (it took me a month). And once you DO start seeing them, you would never want to stop meditating.

After my initial six months (of doing meditation), I stopped, thinking that the effects must be permanent now. Within a week, I noticed a sharp decline in my concentration, self-control, mood, and thought clarity.

When I am meditating regularly, I can easily focus on a single task for hours. Time flies by without me noticing. While writing this book, I was able to write continuously for four-five hours without getting distracted. I also found that I could ignore negative thoughts and fully concentrate on the end result.

Let me share another example. I wanted to make my book, *Success Habits of High Achievers*, the best possible resource anybody could find on the topic of success. But several times, negative thoughts would take over:

"Maybe it's not as good as I thought."

"Who am I to write a book? I have never done it before."

"It will never reach people who need it."

"It's a waste of time."

During this phase, meditation gave me internal strength. It helped me regain my composure and focus. I said to myself, "no, it is good." and "There are people who need it, and I'll make sure they get their hands on it."

I would even say that if it wasn't for meditation, I wouldn't be able to finish the book.

I highly, highly recommend taking 15 minutes of your time and do meditation. Its profound benefits will help you tremendously in ALL areas of your life.

2. Pay complete attention to the present activity

When doing your day-to-day activities, be more aware of the environment around you. Really look at things. I mean it. Really look at them. Notice small details like colors, shape, weight, taste, smell, shine, etc.

This will allow you to cultivate present moment awareness. When coupled with daily meditation practice, your mind will not wander. You will feel the difference. In about ten days, you'll start noticing things you ignored in the past because you are now paying attention.

Really looking and engaging in an activity will shut down your thoughts, and time will seem to fly-by. Do you remember the last time you were engaged in your favorite hobby and hours went away like minutes? That was the power of being present in the moment.

Because you like that activity, you are paying complete attention to it. You are present to the moment with no thoughts & worries. Time flies by. After you finish that activity, you feel energized and peaceful.

The good news is, when you learned to be in the present moment, you would feel like this after every activity you do.

3. Be aware of your thoughts

This concept is from a mindfulness meditation technique. Basically, you start paying attention to the thoughts that are going on in your brain, NON-JUDGMENTALLY. Do not label any thoughts good or bad. Just observe them objectively. You will notice that thoughts are coming from a 'different' source.

It is not YOU who is thinking. Rather the thoughts are generating from somewhere else. You and your thinking mind are separate entities. This concept plays a very important role in allowing you to separate yourself from your thoughts.

You no longer identify yourself with your thoughts. You can clearly see that you and your thinking mind are different, so you stop taking ownership of your negative thoughts. It is not you who is thinking. You are a separate entity. So when you are different from your thinking mind, you have the option of not listening to your thoughts. You may hear them, but do not pay them any importance. This makes it easier for you to stop giving un-needed attention to your negative thoughts.

This may not be-all-end-all for being present but can be a great starting point. Try this one.

4. Minimize activities that stop you from being present

One of the best ways to be more present is to minimize activities that make your brain dull & unable to focus on the present. Some activities make you present, and some don't. If you aim to become more present, then gradually remove activities that are not helping that goal.

Activities like watching TV, playing video games, drinking alcohol, taking drugs, etc., are some of the ways people 'numb' their brain to the present moment. Instead of facing deeper issues, they try to find happiness by escaping reality.

What these people don't realize is that running away from the present moment will never make them truly happy. They might feel good momentarily, but they will never feel 'satisfied.' Running away will never solve anything. Only when you start embracing the present moment and face deeper issues will you feel content.

What's so scary is that these activities are so deeply ingrained in our society that they are considered good... even luxury by some people. But since we intend to become more present at the moment, it is imperative that we gradually minimize or completely remove these activities from our daily life. It will allow your daily lifestyle to help you become more present.

"Always hold fast to the present moment in every situation. Every moment is of infinite value, for it is the representative of a whole eternity." -- **Johann Von Goethe.**

Positive Energy Principle #6

GRATITUDE - GIVE AND RECEIVE JOY EVERY DAY

There's a saying, "*when we get old, we'll look back at our life and smile.*"

Why wait? We can start right now.

The practice of gratitude proposes a daily reflection on overlooked aspects of our lives which we should be grateful for. In this fast-paced world, it's easy to lose touch with what really matters in life, things we are already blessed with.

The endless chase for happiness spans over the entire course of our life, only to realize in the end, we always had what we were searching for. The joy, peace, and content we desperately wanted was inside our hearts from the very beginning.

Nothing external can provide true, lasting happiness.

Sadly, such a profound realization normally occurs at later stages of life. We always have a choice. At any moment, we can choose to be happy and grateful.

Gratitude provides comfort in difficult times and supports us in changing the course of our lives. It's a progressive journey towards lasting inner peace and joy.

Gratitude is a gift. It warms the heart, lightens our load, and brightens the day. We can feel it anywhere, at any time, and it's free. Gratitude embodies love, joy, contentment, happiness, and peace. It has one of the highest vibrational fre?uencies. It is the gateway to love.

Alluding to the fast-paced lifestyle we have right now, it's easy to forget things we have in our life that we are thankful for.

There is a law of familiarity in human psychology that says, "we tend to devaluate things over time that are so precious in our life." As time passes, we tend to pay less importance to the valuable things, people, and experiences we have in life. It's easy to forget how blessed we are.

Gratitude is the practice of being thankful for all that we are blessed with. When we are stuck in the hamster wheel of chasing money, achievements, and accolades, we fail to realize the importance of what we already have.

We are truly blessed to live in an era like this. Some people say if I become too thankful for the things I already have in my life, I will feel content, and it will decrease my motivation to achieve greater goals.

That is simply not correct. Gratitude is not about you losing drive or motivation to achieve. Gratitude is about going for what you want in life with feelings of thankfulness in your heart.

"I am blessed. I already have enough to be grateful for. Let's take this to another level."

It's not about gratitude vs. drive. It is about *achieving happily.*

When you have a sense of thankfulness in your heart, you don't feel as afraid. Failures, setbacks do not affect you as much because you know you have been blessed with several wonderful things already. If you look closely, your life is already great. It's all about *focus* - what you look at when you observe your life.

Everything has an upside and downside. It all depends on where you look. Do you focus on positive or negative?

Gratitude is a *deliberate practice* that makes us focus on the good things in life. It focuses on the things we should be thankful for.

And this is a daily practice, not just a mindset or a one-time thing. It's easy to forget how wonderful your life is when you are working nonstop in the fast-paced life we have today. Nobody sits down to think about the things they are thankful for. Everybody is chasing accolades, money, fame, achievements...wanting more, more, and more.

We think all of our achievements will make us happy when we finally attain them in the future. It never happens. The high you get after achieving something is short-lived. After a few days or months, you can hardly feel excited about what you accomplished. You just feel the same as before you achieved it.

After a lot of trial and error, we finally conclude that all that we wanted was inside us the entire time. We were chasing phantoms for the whole time.

Eternal Source of Peace & Joy

Amid the clutter in our mind and demands on our time, it is important to learn how to have peace in our lives. It starts with an attitude of gratitude. There is always something in your life to be thankful for at the end of the day. There is always something to look forward to at dawn of each new day.

Stop thinking of the shortfalls of life. This clutters our mind. It serves no purpose.

For many years now, I start and end my day with prayers of gratitude. The sun does not always shine. Life does not hum all the time - but it does not mean that the melody is lost or gone. It is just interrupted.

It only takes a few minutes to say a brief prayer of gratitude each day upon waking up. I am thankful for seeing another day. Many are languishing in hospitals or private homes praying for a bit more time on earth.

It does not matter that there are days when things don't work out as planned. Focus on what worked and what went well. Never start the day with thoughts of what could go wrong. This is directing the Universe to louse up your day.

Thoughts are energy. Positive thoughts project powerful positive vibrations around you. Express your gratitude from the deep of your heart. Taking a few moments to say a prayer of gratitude brings calmness, makes panic recede to oblivion.

Even in troubled times, be thankful for the blessings of the Universe. Be thankful for the love given and shared. Be thankful for the beauty that surrounds you. Mistakes are blessings in disguise, stepping stones to find strength and courage to pick up the pieces as you walk along your path.

Effect of gratitude on your social life

Having a sense of gratitude brings a lot of joy and satisfaction to our life. It enables us to look outwards, to how other people are feeling.

It's hard to be empathic towards others when we are distracted by our inner turmoil. Gratitude frees up our mental energy to focus on how other people are feeling. We can only pour water into other's cups when we have some in our own. When we are too caught up with our problems, it's difficult to be empathic.

The practice of gratitude fills up our cup (of positive emotions) and gives us the ability to focus outwards, on understanding & making things better for others.

Empathy and gratitude are extremely important. In our society, we teach life skills, decision-making skills, and goal setting to prevent substance abuse, gang activity & juvenile delinquency. Empathy and gratitude are very critical as well.

An article from New York Parenting talks about these skills. Gratitude (self focused) is when a person focuses on the positives in their life, which can result in increased happiness, optimism, satisfaction, and lack of stress.

Empathy (other-centered) is when you see life through the lens of others, which is an important skill in building healthy relationships. These skills are some of the greatest predictors for how successful a person would be in the 21st century.

Unfortunately, many people today lack these skills. An article from Scientific American analyzes a study that concludes almost 75 percent of youth today rate themselves as less empathic than the average youth 30 years ago.

Empathy and gratitude have a positive impact on all our personal and professional relationships. Problems of abuse, depression, crime, suicide and a host of other problems would likely decrease if human beings increased their dosages of empathy. Conversely, the absence of empathy and gratitude can lead to negative results. Empathy spread among all people in all environments can make the difference between depression and joy in everyday life. Empathy could well be the strongest get-well treatment for our society.

Empathy involves understanding other person's feelings on a specific matter, in addition to their background that brought them to this point. Empathy involves suspending any judgments toward other person's feelings until they are understood accurately. True empathy requires an attempt to become one with the other individual.

The language of empathy is the language of gratitude and respect. The respect comes in the form of wording (telling people how you will act, not how they have to act), and tone of voice. Sarcasm and putdowns are never an acceptable part of empathy; when another person tries to control a person in this way, it usually backfires. When an adult expresses empathy, there is no negative for youth to react to.

Effect of gratitude on relationships

Are you taking your partner for granted OR, even worse, focusing on what she/he isn't doing or saying? If you wish your partner would change, and have already asked, pleaded or begged for these changes to be made, it's time to stop. Not only will this fails to bring about the changes you desire, but it will actually hurt your relationship! Instead of focusing on what is wrong in your relationship, take time to appreciate what's right. It would dramatically improve the way you feel about your partner AND your relationship.

Lot of us take our partner (and our relationship) for granted. Our significant other is just 'there'; living alongside of us and doing whatever they do. Or maybe it goes beyond taking him/her for granted. Maybe you're locked in conflict, and actively dislike your partner. You may be reading this and thinking, "Gratitude and appreciation?! For MY partner? No way! Not when she/he doesn't.

For many people, it takes a crisis to feel how important our loved one really is to us. It may be only after we lose someone that we realize how precious they were. When we are in touch with the sanctity of life, it can shift the way we feel about our loved ones. We recognize their importance and feel more appreciative. For some, the crisis could be an illness. I've heard cancer survivors (shockingly) say that they are grateful for their illness because it made them feel grateful for the relationships they already have.

But it doesn't have to take illness or loss for you to learn to appreciate your partner. You don't have to continue to live mindlessly, without really being present for all the goodness that already exists in your relationship. A shift in your thinking or a change in what you decide to notice can dramatically affect the way you feel. In partnerships, shifting HOW you see your partner will absolutely affect how you feel in your relationships AND will affect the relationship itself.

Let's shift how you see your partner. What do you feel grateful for about who your partner is? What is good about him/her just as he/she is? What do you love about...

- His/her strengths?

- His/her looks and appeal?

- Special or simple, but beautiful, things he/she does or says?

- His/her character or personality?

Was this a shift for you? Do you allow yourself to see your partner's strengths? How would things change if you could open your eyes to the positive aspects of this person? What if you could then express your gratitude to her/him?

It's likely that you've waited, asked, begged, and pressured your partner to change. How successful has that been for you? My guess is not very. While it would be nice if our partner were to change to become exactly what we'd like him/her to be, it's not likely to happen, no matter how much we beg. Instead, transformation comes from your choice to see, think and do things differently. It's you. You hold the tools to transform your relationship. Acknowledging your partner's strengths is one of these tools.

How can you acknowledge what you are grateful for about your partner?

- Tell him/her what you notice, especially at the moment you notice it.

- Thank him/her with spoken word, written word, or touch.

- Decide NOT to include a reference to a time he/she wasn't like that.

- Be an advocate for your partner by telling others what's good about him/her.

- Give a prayer of thanks for having this person in your life.

- Giving thanks for the goodness that exists will transform you, the relationship, and, ultimately, your partner.

Effect of Gratitude on Emotional Health

If you've experienced gratitude or appreciation for someone or something, chances are you felt all warm and fuzzy with it. You know the feeling - all is right with the world, and you're on the very top of it. When you felt that way, you were experiencing what positive psychology experts (the happiness scientists) refer to as "flow" or being "in the zone"... via gratitude high. Gratitude: turns out it is one drug that's really good for you. And it has guaranteed side-effects that are hard to beat; it can make you happier and healthier too.

The Institute of HeartMath reports that scientists now have ways to measure the effects of gratitude on our well-being and when they did, they found something amazing going on:

"According to to research at IHM, true feelings of gratitude, appreciation and other positive emotions can synchronize brain and heart rhythms, creating a bodywide shift to a scientifically measurable state called coherence. In this optimal state, the body's systems function more efficiently, generating a greater balance of emotions and increased mental clarity and brain function."

Balanced emotions, mental clarity, regulated heart rate - all that adds up to a happier, healthier you. And how wonderful is it that just counting your blessings can help put you there?

Better still, there are some nice side effects. The biochemical changes that gratitude triggers more DHEA, the anti-aging hormone, and boost the immune system, so we look younger & feel healthier, just from consciously feeling grateful.

Studies also found that practicing daily gratitude exercises lifted people's spirit overall. The benefit was compounded by thinking these thoughts frequently because the heavy traffic of grateful thoughts racing along neural pathways of brain makes the path smoother for future grateful thoughts to travel, the same way a well-used trail in the woods makes it easier and faster for subsequent hikers. So loses those little gratitude trailblazers and get ready for a happier, healthier you.

A positive outlook towards life

Practicing gratitude will change your outlook to a positive one. When you daily remind yourself how blessed you already are, your perception will shift. You will start focusing on the good things life has to offer. You will look for what's good and wonderful.

This change will shift the course of your life. You will experience more positivity and joy. It will lead to several more experiences that you would become grateful for. It's an upward cycle of positivity with you going up and up and up.

More peaceful and relaxed

Another powerful effect of practicing gratitude daily is that you will become more peaceful and relaxed. When you focus on all that is good in your life, you will feel less anxious about the future. You will feel at ease with your being.

You will be more willing to accept yourself and your life. You will be at peace with all that you have, and no matter what society tells us, you will feel content and comfortable in your own skin. I love this feeling.

More forgiving

As you practice gratitude, you will be more forgiving toward others. If somebody wronged you in the past, you would be more likely to forgive them and move on. The reason behind this is the fact that every day you remind yourself of things that are great in your life, and you feel extremely thankful.

This feeling of gratitude burns away any negativity that we have experienced in the past. It changes your mindset and the way of thinking that minor setbacks and negative experiences do not affect you as much.

You recover faster from an insult or cheating and are far more likely to forgive other people and move on.

Increased confidence

Can you imagine how confident you would feel if you are reminded of all the wonderful things you already have in your life?

Practicing gratitude increases your overall confidence in life. Back up by the reminders of the positive memories that already exist in your life, you will feel unstoppable. There will be a sense of satisfaction and pride in your steps. You feel more content and are not affected by the things that could go wrong.

More social and outgoing

With increased confidence and a relaxed demeanor, you will become a more social and outgoing person. You will have increased tolerance for the differences between people and be more likely to open up to their ideas.

When a person practices gratitude, he emits an aura of positive emotions and optimism that people find very attractive. In the world that we live in today, people are drawn towards a positive, confident person.

Resiliency against setbacks and criticism

People who practice gratitude are more resilient against criticism and setbacks. Daily reminders of how wonderful their life is, makes them much more resistant to negativity and negative experiences. Such people bounce back from setbacks faster.

When you experience positive emotions daily, your mind shifts predominantly towards positivity. In other words - your mind becomes habitual to positivity and resistant to negativity. You become biased towards positivity. Wow, who doesn't want that?

How to Practice Gratitude Every Day?

1. Deliberately think and say the magic words, "thank you."

2. The more you deliberately think and say the magic words, "thank you", the more gratitude you feel.

3. The more gratitude you deliberately think and feel, the more abundance you receive.

Expressing gratitude can help you achieve your dream life. Sit down with a computer or pen & paper and make a list of what you really want in every area of your life.

Think through every detail of what you want to be, do, or have in your life - in your relationships, career, finances, health and every area that are important to you.

You can be as specific and detailed as you like but remember your job is simply to list what you want. The "how" will be done for you when gratitude works its magic.

If you want a better job or your dream job, then think about everything you want the job to be. Get very clear about what you want in the job by thinking it through thoroughly and writing all the details down.

If you want money to educate your children, work out the details of their education, including which school you want them to attend and the cost so that you know exactly how much money you will need.

If you want to travel, write down the details of the countries you want to visit, what you want to see and do, where do you want to stay, and how you want to travel.

If you want more health, be specific about what ways you want to improve you health and body. If you want a dream home, list every detail of what you want the home to be, room by room. If there are specific material things you want, like a car, clothes, or appliances, write them down.

If you want to achieve a goal in sports, getting a degree, be a writer, actor, or have your own business, write it down and be specific as possible.

Write down the little things, the big things, and what you want this moment, this month, or this year. As you think of more things, add them to the list, and as you receive things, cross them off the list. An easy way is to divide the list into categories:

Health and body

Career and work

Money

Relationships

Personal desires

Material things

When you get clear about the things you want, you are giving a definite direction to the way you want gratitude's power to change your life, and you are ready to begin the most exciting and thrilling adventure you've ever been on.

"*When I started counting my blessings, my whole life turned around.*" -- Willie Nelson

When you are grateful for the things you have, no matter how small they may be, you will begin to notice an increase in the number of things you can be grateful for. If you are grateful for the money you have, however little, you will see your money magically grow. If you are grateful for a relationship, you will see it miraculously get better.

To start this practice, first thing in the morning, make a list of ten blessings in your life you are grateful for. Write why you're grateful for each blessing. If you show gratitude every day, your life will change.

"*Live the law of attraction by being grateful and expressing your gratitude to others consistently with others.*" - Kody Bateman.

Daily gratitude exercises

Finding ways to experience and practice gratitude has shown to be one of the most powerful predictors of happiness and well-being.

How easy is it for you to find gratitude in your own life? Can you readily name people, places, and experiences you are thankful for? How often do you take time to step back and really appreciate what you have?

Increasing number of studies show that doing simple exercises like writing a thank you letter or creating a gratitude list have shown to improve positive emotions and decrease stress & anxiety.

The best past is that these "gratitude exercises" take very little time and are really simple & easy to do.

There are several practices out there, but here I am providing mindsets and exercises that I believe are best for feeling grateful.

1. Grateful for the people and love you have in your life

It's very important to feel grateful for the people you have in your life that love you or support you. Set aside 10 minutes in your day and sit down with a piece of paper and pen. Write down at least ten times you felt grateful for the people that have touched your life.

Be grateful for all the people that you had in the past who have a great influence on your life. Remind yourself of the love, the connection, and the bond that you had.

If you are fortunate enough to still have people that have positively impacted your life, you are very blessed. A lot of us don't have people in our lives today that love & support us.

 Remind yourself of experiences that you have shared, the laughs, the pain, the love... everything. Remind yourself.

Never forget even for a moment how blessed you are to have experienced such wonderful people who loved and care for you. Most of the people in the world would do anything to have the bond, the connection in their life like you had.

Thank god or the universe for connecting you with such wonderful people and giving you so many loving, wonderful moments.

I always end it with "thank you for everything... (their name or relation with you)"

2. Grateful for the money and possessions

50% of the world population lives under the spending of 2 dollars per day. If you have the time, money, and resources to read this book right now, you are very fortunate.

We don't think of ourselves as blessed financially because we compare ourselves with richer people. We never think of how fortunate we are to be born in a society where you get education, welfare, and support from your family or friends.

We fail to look at the contrast. So many people are living under constant threat of terrorism. Millions of people have no source of education, healthy food, and even shelter.

Look around you. You have so many things at your disposal. A home, a table, a fan, a sofa, a TV, computer, fridge, and hundreds of valuable things that we never pay any importance to. Look at them and think about billions of people around the world who don't have what you have right now.

It's ok to look at wealthy people and be driven to become better financially. But simultaneously, look at what you have right now and be thankful for that.

You are already much better off than a big portion of the world's population. Be thankful for what you have.

3. Grateful for your health and body

We should be extremely grateful to the universe for giving us this body and form. In all the species on planet earth, we have a unique gift among all. We have consciousness. We can think. We can realize what is going on around us and how we are feeling.

We can notice our thoughts. We can feel our bodies and have a perspective of what is going on in our life. The human body is a marvel of nature. Even the best scientists in the world are unable to replicate the human body in the form of machines.

The body you have right now is perfect. It is a result of billions of years of evolution, and over all this time, nature has continued to evolve and perfect it.

You are so lucky to have what you take for granted - our body, our mind, and our health.

That is the unique gift we have. People can have everything as same as you, but there will never be another you. In the billions of humans living on earth, there is no one else who has your body and mind.

You are unique among billions. You have a choice to act on free will and can choose to express yourself as you want.

We never look at ourselves from this perspective. Because of the law of familiarity, we tend to not pay importance to our most valuable aspect - our body & mind.

Observe yourself right now. Look at your hands, legs, shoulder. See your whole body in the mirror and say, "thank you... for giving me this body".

Ask a person who is suffering from a brain problem or missing an arm. They will tell you the importance of having a healthy body and mind. You are very fortunate to walk on two legs, hold things with your hands, stand straight with the help of your spine, eat and breathe properly...

There are millions of people who cannot do those things. Some have unfortunately lost their legs in an accident. Some were born with physical and mental disabilities. If you are healthy and have a healthy brain and body, you should be extremely grateful for what you have.

Cherish yourself. Don't let the law of familiarity devaluate the importance of having a healthy body and mind. Say thank you every time you look in the mirror at yourself.

4. Grateful for your memories and experiences

Like your body, you are also unique in the way that nobody on earth has the same life experiences and memories of those experiences as you. The things you have been through, what you felt, what you saw, what you thought, are some of the most valuable aspects of yourself which no one else on earth shares exactly.

Your past experiences have a great impact on the perspective you have on life. How do you think people are, what is valuable to you? People in your life and the memories you have of them - sweet or bitter - all of them are unique. They made you the person who you are today. Be thankful for your past experiences and memories.

Look back at your life, and you will find such amazing experiences, such valuable experiences that are irreplaceable in this life. If you had someone who loved you, or you push your limits & achieved something greater, or you did something special for someone, or they did something for you... cherish those memories.

You are very fortunate to have the memories that you have. I know the past is full of sweet and bitter memories, but all of them are yours, and I believe till the time we don't experience bad emotions, we cannot put in perspective how valuable good experiences are.

Good, bad, everything is valuable. Everything is an experience. Everything is YOU.

Be grateful for all of it.

Some people would give up anything to experience the memories you have. Look back at your life and never forget the moments you have experienced. You have one life, and there is only one person like you in the whole world. Be proud of yourself. Cherish your life. Cherish special moments of your life.

Whenever you think back at those special memories and smile, say "thank you."

5. Grateful for the world around you

Look around you with optimism, and you will find the world full of possibilities and opportunities all around you. We are blessed to be living in a world that has evolved so much that you can talk right now to a person sitting on the opposite part of the globe.

It used to take years to communicate like that in the past. Right now, we have the best time to prosper, or start a business, or achieve success than ever before in history. With the abundance of knowledge available at your fingertips at every moment, you are only limited by your imagination and creativity.

The world is filled with so many incredible opportunities that you have to only decide what you want to do and go for it. Be thankful for the fact that you don't have to conform to the whims of a lord or king. You have your own free will. Never in the history of man ever had we this kind of opportunities.

The world around us also provides us with food to eat, shelter to live in, and air for breathing. We pay no attention to all of these because these things are "already there." But when we stop and think that all of these - food, shelter, or air is limited, we feel a deep sense of appreciation for the fact that we have all these in our life.

Our world is just a dot in the expansion of our galaxy, and till the millions of light-years, no place has air, food, and shelter. Our earth is a marvel of creation and a jewel of the universe. More than 99.99% of our universe is dead and empty with no life, air, food, or hospitable environment. We only have our tiny earth. This is our home. This is the only place we have. This is the only place we can live in.

Be grateful for it. We live on a beautiful planet, filled with green mountains, deep blue oceans, fertile plains, and such a diverse type of life all around. This is our home... and it's gorgeous. Take time in the future and travel the world to see the place we live in. This is our home. This is your home. Would you not want to look at it? Would you not want to be thankful for it?

In summary:

- Look for the opportunities to say "Thank You" more often during your day.

- Write down 5 people you are grateful for (and why).

- Write down 5 experiences you are grateful for (and why).

- Write down 5 things about yourself you are grateful for (and why).

- Give back to your community through volunteer work or charity.

- Visualize how your life would be without certain things you take for granted (food, shelter, warmth, relationships).

- Send a "Thank You" letter or e-mail towards someone who has really helped you in the past.

- Create a piece of music, art, or poetry - and dedicate it to someone.

- Keep an eye out for the simple pleasures of life.

- I call this shared gratitude. Find someone; a best friend is good for this, who also wants to increase their gratefulness. Sit in chairs facing each other, kitchen or dining room chairs work well, within touching distance. One of you starts and expresses something you are grateful for, and then the other partner does the same, back and forth, back and forth. You will find that you feed off each other's ideas.

All of these exercises are easy. However, when you take the time to actually practice them, they can make a dramatic improvement in your everyday life.

Do you feel you need more gratitude in your life? Then schedule 5-10 minutes every morning and night to practice any of the gratitude exercises we covered.

Today, more and more people are taking advantage of practicing gratitude like this to improve the state of their lives.

Often times, we struggle with happiness because we are constantly striving for more. We believe, once we have X or Y, we'll finally be happy - but this is rarely ever the case.

The key to happiness is to learn how to be happy with what we already have - no matter what it is or where we find ourselves in our life. Gratitude helps you to grow, brings joy & laughter into your life and the lives of all those around you.

"As we express our gratitude, we must never forget that the highest appreciation is not to utter words, but to live by them." - **- John F. Kennedy.**

FORGIVENESS - THE PATH TO EMOTIONAL FREEDOM

Did you know that a spring can have a memory? It's true. If you place weight on a spring and you leave that weight on the spring for a while, the spring may not return to its original strength or form.

The same thing can be seen in a piece of paper. My brother folds the top-right corner of pages in books – this drives me nuts. Once a page has been folded, it retains a crease. The page keeps a memory of the fold.

People can be much the same. We, too, retain memories of events or stresses that weigh on us like the spring or crease us like the folded pages of a book. Events in our lives create memories, and in some instances, they create scars – very sensitive reminders or memories.

Because your bad memory will have strong negative emotions fixed to it, every time you think or talk about your bad experience, you will also bring about and activate all emotional responses which will trigger stressful symptoms in your body.

While it's perfectly normal to feel bad about an unpleasant experience, we may end up holding on to these negative feelings for a time longer than necessary.

The longer we hold on to bitter feelings, the more power and influence they get over us.

However bad your experience was, whatever happened to you is hopefully now over. If you think about it, you will see that the danger, fear, and negativity now only exist in your mind and your perceptions.

Do not let stories of the past control your present and future.

Forgiveness is a choice

At any moment, we have a choice. We can either hold on to anger, or we could let it go. Forgiveness is a healing process that liberates you from unpleasant memories of the past.

Nearly everyone has been hurt by the actions or words of another. Perhaps your parents criticized your learning skills, or your colleague sabotaged a project, or your partner had an affair. Such wounds can leave you with lasting feelings of anger, bitterness, or even vengeance.

But if you don't practice forgiveness, you might be the one who pays most dearly.

When you forgive, you are doing something powerful for yourself. When you hang on to it, it becomes a part of your baggage. It affects everything you do. It damages relationships. You see, choosing not to forgive is the definition of bitterness. Being a bitter person is living a miserable life.

Being able to forgive requires empathy, compassion, kindness, and understanding. It also requires you to accept that forgiveness is a choice you always have.

Forgiveness is not forgetting

Forgiving does not mean forgetting. I know that's what you have always heard. Passages from the Bible states that God remembers our sins no more and throws them away.

That's what God does, but we are not God. Being a human, we are not capable of erasing something from our memory as if it never happened. And neither are we told to. That's not a prerequisite of forgiveness. So quit thinking you have not forgiven someone because the memory of it pops into your head at times.

Forgiveness is healing

Forgiveness is a crucial component to your personal development because when you forgive, you let go of what you do not want in your life and focus on what you do want.

"*To forgive is like setting a prisoner free and realizing that prisoner was you*" - Lewis B. Smedes.

Some people choose not to forgive because of what they believe forgiveness does for the other person.

A common statement I hear is, "This person hurt me, and I will never forgive them for what they did to me." I want to stress that the recipient of your forgiveness is not as important as the healing effect that you will receive when you let go of your hurt and pain and forgive them of their wrongdoings.

When you hold thoughts of hate, anger, and resentment towards another person, place, or situation, those are the same emotions that you will experience in your life.

For example, if I am giving off emotions of anger and resentment towards someone because of their wrongdoings, then at the time of expression, I am actually angry and resentful. As long as I express anger and resentment towards someone else, I will remain angry and resentful.

I am not advocating that any person - who had been the recipient of harm - should be ignored, nor do I mean that they should not express any emotional response. I am saying that there is healing in forgiveness.

When you release all of the negative emotions that you have attached to a person, place or situation and focus on forgiveness, then you will be able to experience joy in its fullness.

Realize that you do not have to be in the same room with a person to forgive them. You can give thoughts of forgiveness to a person as well as pray that they will be changed for the better.

Praying for forgiveness is not a one-time event. Forgiveness needs to be practiced every day. The reason forgiveness needs to be practiced every day is because each day there is a possibility that you are holding on to a negative thought that needs to be released.

There is no point dwelling on past experiences in which you have placed the blame on yourself. Everyone makes mistakes, and you are no different. Today, allow yourself a clean slate, a clean record, a forgiven past.

Only when you forgive yourself and others can you attain true freedom.

Your ego may stop you

Your ego may stop you from forgiving another person.

When we think about forgiveness, it may seem like an impossible task at first. We think, "I'm angry. I'm hurt. I'm offended. Why should I have to forgive? I'm the injured party!"

The problem with avoiding forgiveness is that it is detrimental to our healing. For my whole life, I have seen what goes around, comes around. I know I have made countless blunders in my life - conscious and unconscious - and I always expect to be forgiven. So it is only right that I should forgive others.

It may be surprising to learn that we can benefit greatly from forgiving others. In fact, we benefit far more than those we forgive. Studies show that people who forgive are happier and healthier than those who hold resentments.

This information is not new. Buddhism views forgiveness as a practice to prevent harmful thoughts from causing havoc on one's mental wellbeing. Buddhism recognizes that feelings of ill-will leave a lasting effect on our mind; they called it "karma." And Judeo-Christian philosophy places great importance on forgiveness as a path to redemption.

We don't need to hold grudges, desires to harm others... because nothing we do to harm/punish them would heal our wounds. Healing will only come from forgiveness.

Holding hatred inside you is the worst thing you can do for yourself. If you hold a grudge against someone, your hatred towards them is not only keeping a connection between you and them but also strengthening it.

To let off the emotional baggage we carry in our hearts, we must forgive the person responsible. As long as you keep anger in your heart, you will always be connected to the past, to that person and those memories.

Holding on to the past puts you in a victim mindset. If you do not go ahead and forgive those people or events, you will essentially live those moments every day of your life. I did too. Please let it go. For your own sake. We deserve better.

And by forgiving, we are not just giving a gift of forgiveness to other people. It's a gift to ourselves. Forgiving will break the emotional shackles that bound us. If we wish to live life on our own terms and with free will, forgiving the past is the answer.

To live a life of positivity and inner peace, you must forgive what happened in the past and move on. This whole chapter is about how to do that.

Why should you forgive?

First of all, you need to come up with a reason to forgive the other person/event. Why would you need to forgive and move on with your life? What will happen if you don't?

Identify the pain you are feeling in your day-to-day life. How much do you want to be free from it?

In what ways do you think the past is controlling your present and future? What is it that is costing you right now emotionally, financially, relationship-wise?

The idea is to come up with a reason why you NEED to forgive the past that carries a lot of importance to you. The key here is 'importance.' The reasons you come up with must make you go

"YES! I want to move on! This is really bothering me! I must move on!"

When you come up with strong reasons for why you need to forgive and move on, half of the battle is over. You have taken a huge step towards living a life of peace and tranquility. Your reasons will drive you to think differently.

If you were cursing what happened in the past when you thought about it, now you will try to focus on why you need to let it go.

Please take some time to dig deep within yourself and come up with important reasons why you should forgive what happened in the past.

And you do not even have to agree with what happened to you was right, or the person who did you wrong is innocent. Forgiveness is not about being right or wrong. It is about letting go...

"I don't agree with what you did, but I forgive you anyway..."

This is forgiveness.

You don't *have* to see things from their perspective. You can still forgive them for what happened.

"I forgive you anyway..."

We think it was personal

Most of the time, the real hurt comes from thinking that the other person knew us, knew what we were thinking, who we really were, our life situation, our goals, our dreams, our aspirations. We thought another **person** knew everything about us, and even then, they did that horrible thing.

We take it as a personal attack against us. It's not the case. No one else, especially people who wronged you in the past, REALLY knew where you were coming from. Even if they belonged to your family, they did not know who you really were.

Think about it.

Do you really think the people who wronged you knew everything about you? Who were you? Where were you coming from? What did you think? Your values? Your emotions? Your hopes and desires?

Nope.

They didn't know anything.

For them, you were one of the strangers who come across their path. Even if they knew you, it was only superficially. This was not a malicious, personal attack. You were not their lifelong purpose. It was not personal.

We make it personal in our mind because we have very little information about what really was going through THEIR head. We never got to see things from their perspective. We conjured up a story in our minds that they knew EVERYTHING about us and then proceeded to go ahead and harm us.

Realize this fact and pay close attention to the story you made up in your mind about why it all happened. If you try, you will find evidence that proves things are not as you thought they happened.

For everything that happens, there could be millions of possibilities behind it. And we could never be sure of what was the cause. We can only speculate in our minds.

The main point is not to take what happened in the past as a personal attack against your own self. It was not. More than likely, those people did not know you at all. It was not personal.

Let go of that anger. As long as you keep the hate inside you, you will experience those negative emotions on a daily basis. That is not how we would like to live our life.

Life is just too precious and short to live like this. Let it go. Or it will keep circulating in your head for the rest of your life, which is what we don't want.

Another reason to let go of the past is that you got to learn a very valuable lesson from it. There is an old saying, "that which doesn't kill you... makes you stronger." You have learned a very valuable lesson that could serve you for the rest of your life. Maybe it happened because you were to learn a valuable lesson from it and make some big from it in the future.

You could help other people in avoiding similar experiences. You could use what you learned to reach new heights in your finances, relationships, health in the future. There are always two sides to a coin. There are upsides and downsides to everything in life.

You are the one who decides which one to focus on. The world is harsh if you look for evidence of that. The world is full of joy and beauty if you choose to focus on that.

The absolute best thing about this is that you have the choice. You have the power to decide your perspective and the course of your life. Universe has given you the most valuable gift in all existence - Consciousness. And you decide whether you will use it for positive or negative.

You have the power to change the meaning of anything that happens in life. An event itself is neither good nor bad. We feel bad about something because we give it a negative meaning. When we give something a positive meaning, it makes us feel good.

For example, it's raining outside. You can look at it and feel bad, "What horrible weather. It will be so inconvenient to go outside."

OR you could give a positive meaning to the rain, "Hey, it's raining outside. I don't have to go out now. Let's finish the book I bought last week. I didn't have the chance to read it much."

See the difference in our perspective.

The event - rain - itself is neutral. It is neither good nor bad. We give meaning to it. Anything that happens in life would be positive or negative depending on how to look at it and what meaning we give to it.

That is one of the most critical principles to follow if we want to live a happy and peaceful life. And the best part is you can start from this very moment. And there is no effort OR cost involved. We are already giving meaning to all the events that happen in our life. Think about it. We consciously or subconsciously give meaning to everything that happens around us. We judge it as good or bad. And we have been doing this for such a long time that now we judge things good or bad without even thinking too much about it. It has become a habit for us.

We are already assigning meaning to events. Make sure to assign a positive meaning to the events as much as you can. What has happened will not change. It is best to learn from it and then give a positive meaning to it:

- It's ok. I learned this valuable lesson from it.

- It's ok. Something worse could have happened but didn't.

- It's ok. I will share this with my loved ones and help them avoid similar experiences.

And so on.

We have very limited power to decide what happens in our life, but we have complete control over what that means to us. Take hold of this power and use it. You have been blessed to have this choice. Use it for positive instead of negative.

Forgive yourself

If you made a mistake in the past and now felt hatred towards yourself, then this section is for you. If you did something bad and now hate yourself over it, you will live those memories every day of your life and feel those negative emotions every time you think about it.

That is a very bad place to get stuck emotionally. It's not good for your emotional or physical health. It can make you susceptible to depression and self-hate or physical problems like a headache and body pain.

There is a lot of suffering to be had if we hate ourselves. So, we need to forgive ourselves. It's not easy, because in our minds, what we did was unacceptable. BUT we have to realize that at that moment that we did what we knew best. We were limited by our knowledge, or we didn't have the perspective that we have right now.

We did what we thought made sense at that moment.

Don't beat yourself for it. Everybody makes mistakes. We are all humans, not gods. It's completely normal to make mistakes. Even big ones. Don't beat yourself for it.

If you are suffering now because you genuinely feel bad for what you did, that's enough for now. You realize you made a mistake, and you are apologetic. That is good. You learned from your mistake and will never do it again to anyone else... That is the BEST you could do now.

That is the highest kind of apology there is... that you realize your mistake and are genuinely apologetic for it.

Don't hate yourself now. That is the best anyone can do after making a mistake.

We all make a mistake. Nobody is immune to it. It's just that some people find it easier to forgive themselves while others don't.

Even if you belong to the latter category, you should forgive yourself. No amount of self-pity or hatred will undo what had been done. The best you or anyone in your place can do now is to realize their mistake and be genuinely sorry for it.

I am sure you feel genuinely bad for what you did. Otherwise, you would not be reading this right now. It's ok.

Listen to me.

It's ok.

You did what you knew best at that point in time. It's ok. Forgive yourself. If you harmed someone else, if they could see your inner agony and how bad you feel about what you did... they would have forgiven you too.

If somebody wronged me in the past... and felt horrible and bad to the point of self-hate... I would forgive them too.

Time heals all wounds. But if you get stuck in emotional turmoil because of memories of something you did in the past...it will haunt you forever.

Even the person who suffered loss because of you will forgive you after a period.

Forgive yourself.

You have learned your lesson. You feel bad. You will never do it again with anybody. That is the best you or anyone in your place could do.

It's ok to forgive yourself now.

Forgive others

If you have content in your heart for any person/group of people, then this section is for you.

Everyone makes mistakes. We are all humans. Some mistakes made by us are small. Some are big. If you think what happened to you was extremely bad and should never have happened to anyone else, like rape or murder attempt... I fully agree with you. Such behaviors are not to be tolerated. They should be punished and get what they deserve.

But that does not include the space you have given them in your heart. Even if you love or hate someone, they still hold a place in your mind and heart. You keep them within you in the form of emotions and thoughts, and memories.

You have to let them go. You have to break that link between you and them. So much time has passed. They even got punishment for what they did. There is nothing more to do. Leave them alone. Get them out of your life completely.

They deserve no place in your thoughts, emotions, and memories. Cut all of that out completely from your life. Let go. They got what they deserved. Now it is of no use reliving those memories daily. It will only lead to hurt, pain, and suffering.

 Let them go. They do not deserve a spot in your mind or life. Do not allow them to have even a moment of your life.

Let go of the past and think about what you want in the future. Look at your experience from a different perspective. How could you use your experience to spread goodness and positivity? How would you use your experience never to let anyone else go through that experience? How could you use your realizations to help other people cope up with their reality? Who has gone through the same experience?

No matter how painful the past may be. If you look closely, there is always something you learn from and use it in a positive direction. You can lead your life (as well as the lives of other people) to a bright future... if you truly seek out a way to do that.

You always have a choice. You can either dwell on the past & feel pain for the rest of your life... or you can use your past as a catalyst for a massive change in your life as well as the lives of other people.

The ball is in your court.

In other cases, if somebody wronged you in a non-life-threatening way like cheated on you financially, broke your heart, hide something from you... you may try to forgive them.

Why?

What they did was very bad, but by holding a grudge against them, you will never be fully able to move on with your life.

Even if what they did was very bad, you have to realize that at that time, they did the best thing they knew. From their perspective, they were doing the right thing. They may be completely wrong, but if you hold a grudge against them for a long period, you are doing yourself even more harm.

That is basically your past holding you from experiencing a better present and a better future. Those old memories are blocking you from being happy right now. You are doing more damage to your emotions and life by thinking about the past.

What has happened in the past is over now. It cannot be undone. Accept what happened and learn from it. Make sure you fully grasped what caused it and how you behaved at the time. Learning from bad experiences makes sure it never happens to you or anyone you know.

That which doesn't kill you makes you stronger. It's the truth.

Leave the past behind. After you have learned your lessons from a bad experience, let it go. Otherwise, it will stick with you like glue for the rest of your life. I am sure you don't want that.

We all want to live a peaceful, happy life where we have control over our thoughts and emotions. Know the other way around. It is imperative that you let the past go.

And the way to do that is to forgive the people who wronged you. It may seem hard right now, but later in this chapter, I will share some powerful methods to reduce your anger and calm down your mind. With a calmer mind, it is easier to see the picture from a different perspective and forgive others.

Remember: *All that you resist persists.*

The longer you keep hatred and disdain in your heart, the longer those memories will continue to haunt you.

Forgiveness is the answer, the cure that is needed to get rid of the disease called holding on to negative memories.

How to Calm Your Emotions

If you feel unable to forgive others because the anger or the emotional charge in you is too much, then this will be the section for you. From here, we will be looking at different methods to calm down your inner anger, which will allow you to look at things from a different perspective and be able to forgive others and move on with your life.

Pent-up emotions are carried by tremendous amounts of strength. A person gives a lot of importance to his or her emotions because even if you can't touch emotions, they are very real for the person who experiences them.

We form most of our decisions based on how we are feeling at the time. Sometimes, we use rational thinking and willpower to change how we think and what we do, but most often, emotions determine how we act.

The old words of wisdom "in the battle between heart and mind, it's the heart which always wins" are still the truth.

In order to be able to see things from a different perspective and with an open mind, we need to calm down our powerful emotions that have hijacked our minds.

1. Forgiveness prayer

This is another very effective exercise for allowing ourselves to forgive everyone. I use this simple forgiveness prayer almost daily. It takes only 3-4 minutes and is amazingly effective.

Step 1: Stand in front of a mirror (preferably big enough to see your complete upper body from the waist up). Clasp your hands together in prayer and make sure they are touching your chest.

Step 2: Now look directly in the eyes of your reflection and say out loud, "I FORGIVE (name of the person you wish to forgive or yourself), and I let it go..."

Repeat this 3 or more times.

Step 3: While looking in the eyes of your reflection, say out loud, "I deeply and completely love and accept myself. I forgive everyone."

Repeat this 3 more times.

Notice how relaxed you feel. If there are some negative emotions left, repeat the above steps till negative emotions are completely gone.

2. Forgiveness letter

Another very effective way to let go of the intense emotions trapped inside is to write down all of your thoughts on a blank piece of paper. This is your letter of forgiveness. You can let out everything that you wanted to say to the people who wronged you in the past.

Go all out. Write down all the things you want to say to them and how you really feel inside. Keep expressing until you empty your mind and emotions.

Now you do not have to send this letter. You can go ahead and throw it away after you wrote all that you wanted to say.

Now it cannot be virtual paper (on a computer). This exercise is a lot more effective when done on physical paper and a pen. Writing your thoughts down on a piece of paper has a significant impact on our minds.

One of the reasons we feel rage when we think about bad memories is because there are a lot of unexpressed/suppressed emotions we have inside. As long as we keep holding our thoughts and emotions inside and don't express them, they will turn toxic.

Over time, pent-up emotions tend to get stronger in their intensity which can be very detrimental to our mental and emotional wellbeing.

So write down everything you want to say. Fully express yourself. Nobody is going to see this letter expect you anyway, so go all out. Eventually, you will reach a point where you start feeling calmer. This is the place we wanted to arrive at.

With the newfound calmer mind, write how you would harm your present and future if you keep holding on to the past and write down - "Even though I don't agree with what you did... I forgive you anyway".

Again, don't type it on the computer or mobile. Write all this down on paper. You will immediately start feeling better. You are letting out all the suppressed emotions and thoughts. After you are finished with all of it, you can throw it away if you want.

Your emotions and rage when you think about the past will be severely reduced. And if you repeat this exercise for a few days, you will create a drastic change in how you feel about your past.

Peace, calm, serenity, joy are some of the feelings you will get after doing the above exercises.

This is the magic of forgiveness. It puts the final seal on the past. You will still remember what happened, but the memories will no longer have that old emotional charge.

Forgiving the other person is a wonderful way to free your own self.

You can now choose to forgive. You can now free yourself from the old shackles. You can now forgive any person - whether family, friends, or coworkers - and let go of the past.

You will send out a loud and clear message to the universe that you deserve to experience happiness, love, peace, joy, calm, and freedom.

"When you forgive, you in no way change the past - but you sure do change the future."

3. Meditation raises your inner awareness

To let go of the past and forgive others, you need to get in touch with your inner self. What thoughts do you get when you think about the past? What do you feel? What comes up in your body and mind? How do you react physically?

You have to be aware of how you feel. Only then would you be able to realize how much that inner hatred is blocking you from living a peaceful and happy life. Once you realize how badly these pent-up emotions are harming you, letting them would become a priority for you.

To raise awareness, I would suggest doing meditation for 15-20 minutes every day. Not only will it help you become aware of what's going on inside you... it strengthens you emotionally. You will be more aware of how you feel and be more resistant to negative thoughts that come up.

That is my personal experience. And on top of that, medical science has proved many other benefits of practicing meditation like better self-control, willpower, focus, concentration, calmer and relaxed mind.

It's only a simple breathing exercise that can be done anywhere you want, and there are no obligatory religious connections.

Try meditating for 15-20 minutes every day to calm your emotions and increase your inner awareness.

4. Exercise helps in calming down and feeling better

Along with the prayer, forgiveness letter, and meditation, one more thing I would like to mention that could make a big difference in your emotional health: exercise.

When you move your body during exercise, your body releases a plethora of chemicals that make you feel good inside. It's very common to feel relaxed and peaceful after you have worked out.

This is our biochemistry of the body at work. When you are stressed out, exercise can help you calm down. When you exercise, the body releases "feel-good" chemicals like dopamine and serotonin, which immediately make you feel relaxed and happy.

Clinical studies have proved that exercising has benefits for people who are suffering from depression. This is the extent to which exercising supports our mental & emotional health.

Now, which exercise should you do? Which one is good for you?

The answer is different for different people.

* Brisk walking (walking at a moderate pace, i.e., around 6 km/hr) is something which anyone can do at any age. It's simple, easy, and puts very little stress on the joints, so it is suitable for people of all age groups.

* Heavy exercises like weight lifting and cardio are preferred by younger people and people who are relatively fit already.

* Cycling, swimming, badminton, jumping rope, hiking, and surfing are some of the good exercises that are beneficial for our body and mind.

Everybody is unique so you have to find out which exercise you should do. When deciding upon an exercise, you must take into the account:

* How physically fit are you?

* Which exercises do you like?

* Are you comfortable with the intensity of a chosen exercise?

* Do you have experience with a selected exercise?

Questions like these will give clarity to which exercise you should do. And remember to consult your physician to ensure there's no medical condition stopping you from doing any particular exercise.

When you use the combination of prayer, meditation, exercise, and forgiveness letter, you will start feeling much more relaxed in your day-to-day life. Meditation strengthens you mentally & emotionally.

Exercises make you physically fit and release feel-good chemicals which make you feel better all day, and finally, a prayer & forgiveness letter will release all your trapped thoughts and emotions, which will allow you to think with a much more rational, calmer mind.

Holding a grudge against the past carries a lot of pain for you. If you are not careful, your past will control your present and future life. End this. Let it all go now. Nobody should go through life feeling pain because of something that happened long ago, while I may not know you personally, I can sincerely say: you deserve better.

Forgive the past.

Move on.

GOOD HEALTH - 9 TOP TIPS FOR A HEALTHIER LIFESTYLE

This is a big one! There is a saying - "*you are what you eat.*" The food you eat has a HUGE impact on your brain. Whenever we eat something, certain chemicals are released in the brain depending on the type of food consumed.

For example, consumption of omega-3 fatty acids - found in salmon, walnuts & kiwi fruit - supports synaptic plasticity in the brain and positively affects molecules related to learning and memory that are found in synapses.

Deficiency of omega-3 fatty acids may lead to shorter attention span, unstable mood swings, and even disorders like depression, dyslexia, and dementia.

Diets that are high in saturated fats are becoming recognized for reducing molecules that support cognitive processing and increasing the risk of neurological dysfunction. Link to research: www.ncbi.nlm.nih.gov/pmc/articles/PMC2805706

A lot of times, procrastination, bad mood, feeling down, fear, anxiety, lack of concentration, and unclear thinking can be traced back to our unhealthy diet.

Let me share a personal experience. I used to eat a heavy breakfast in the morning, which included bread, milk, sprouted beans, eggs, etc. I thought it was quite healthy because it contained all the necessary nutrients. But, there was a small problem.

I just couldn't concentrate on work from morning till mid-afternoon. It was like being in a haze. My focus was all over the place. I couldn't think properly. I felt like a thick fog was covering my brain.

After reading a TON of books on the subject, I finally decided to switch to a green shake in the morning. It contained green leafy vegetables, nuts, essential oils, and some fruits. As you can probably guess - it tasted BAD at first, but I experimented with different fruits and got a combination that tasted good.

Now for the important part- from the FIRST DAY I switched from heavy breakfast to a green shake, my mornings got completely transformed. My mind became extremely clear and focused. I could now properly concentrate on an activity without getting disturbed by random negative thoughts. I could now do the same amount of work in half-day that used to take me an entire day.

Sounds amazing, right? It was a revelation for me too. I always knew that healthy food was good for the body and mind but never expected results to be this dramatic.

Bottom line: Watch what you eat. It makes a significant impact!

9 Top Tips for a Healthier Lifestyle

1. Eat more vegetable

Think of food as fuel for the body, and you would want good quality fuel inside your body. Start by adding more fresh fruits and vegetables to your diet. Don't worry too much about cutting down bad foods. I found that if you start adding more healthy food to your diet, the quantity of bad food decreases automatically.

2. Reduce junk food

Reduce your sugar intake as much as you can. Stop eating fried, deep-cooked, or barbecued foods. Try olive oil for cooking. It's a much healthier alternative to normal cooking oils. Make sure you are taking omega-3 oil as well, for its numerous benefits.

3. Add more fiber

Add a green salad with every meal. Eat foods with a low GI, which stabilize your blood sugar and provides energy all day long. Search "low GI foods" in Google for a big list of low GI foods.

4. Go for complex carbohydrates

Eat the right kinds of carbohydrates. Shift from simple carbs (white rice, white bread, white pasta, potatoes) to complex carbs (whole grain pasta, oatmeal, whole grain bread, vegetables, lentils), which break down slowly in the body, giving you a steady flow of energy throughout the day.

5. Find your protein requirement

You don't need much protein. The usually recommended amount is - 0.8 grams per kilogram of your body weight in a day. And while it's possible to get all the 20 different kinds of proteins entirely from plant sources (plenty of info available in books & the Internet), it'll be a bit tough. You can add a small amount of dairy or clean meats like chicken to your main fruits and vegetable diet. This will ensure that you get the whole range of amino acids easily.

6. Focus on nutrition

If you eat a balanced diet with a wide range of fruits and vegetables, there will be enough vitamins and minerals included in your diet. Search online for the recommended quantity of vitamins & minerals per day. You should easily be meeting these requirements if you follow the guidelines above. If not, then consult your doctor for a good vitamin & mineral supplement. Sometimes it does wonders for your health and well-being.

7. Drink enough water

Water makes up about 50-60% of our body. It is inside our cells, blood, tissues, and other parts of the body. A lot of body processes (like sweating) make us lose water fast. Sweating alone can use up to half-liter water in an hour. In extreme weather, that amount can rise to two liters of water consumed in an hour.

Even a 2% decrease in the total water content level of the body reduces our ability to perform at peak mental and physical levels. If you continue to push on without drinking water, you will start getting irritable and tired, along with higher chances of getting muscle cramps.

A 5% decrease in the total water level of the body causes extreme fatigue and drowsiness. It may cause altered vision and tingling sensation in the whole body. 10-15% loss in water levels causes wrinkles on the skin and muscles malfunction. Any loss greater than that is often fatal.

Such is the importance of water for our health. Drink at least 2 to 4 liters of water daily depending on the weather conditions you are living in and the amount of physical activity you do. The more extreme the weather, the more water you need to preserve your water level. Drinking 2 to 4 liters of water is considered safe by many experts. Consult your physician to know exactly how much do you need based on your unique condition.

8. Exercise

It is quite well known that exercise is good for our health. Less known is the TYPE of exercise we need and its duration. Research shows that for most people, a 15-minute brisk walk (walking at around 6 km/hr) is the ideal exercise, as it's not too stressful on the body and pumps up the oxygen flow nicely.

It is one of the few physical activities you can do your whole life. Even older people can take a brisk walk easily. The younger you start, the more benefits you get in the long term. No matter what your age, it's better to start exercising if you aren't already doing so. At a young age, the body can withstand heavy, rigorous physical activities. People in their 20s & 30s usually think about the gym and weight training whenever physical activity is mentioned.

For achieving optimum health, heavy exercises are not necessary. Here are some simple ones which are great for your health:

* Brisk walk

* Cycling at slow speed

* Sweeping or raking outside lawn

* Gardening

* Table tennis

* Painting & plastering

* Heavy house cleaning

* Light dancing

* Push-ups, sit-ups with moderate effort

It all depends on the effort you are willing to make and your physical condition. If you decide to do exercises like walking or cycling, one important point to note is you burn the same number of calories for covering a fixed distance.

For example, if you walk faster for 10 miles, you will burn a lot of calories initially but will slow down afterward. If you walk slowly, you will burn lesser calories but keep doing that longer. In the end, whatever your speed is, you end up burning the same amount of calories for covering a fixed distance. As always, consult your physician before starting any new physical activity.

9. Adequate sleep

One of the most important things for your health is getting enough sleep. When you are well-slept, your mind is much sharper, alert, and resilient. You will have more energy, increased performance, and get a lot more done.

On the other hand, if you lack proper sleep, you will feel drowsy and irritable all day. Your willpower will decrease. Your emotions will be all over the place. Sleep is one of those things which can either make or break your day. It is extremely important to get proper sleep at night.

But how much sleep is enough?

It depends on the individual. Every one of us is unique and has a different sleep requirement. Some people can function normally on 6 hours of sleep while others may need 8-9 hours to feel well-rested.

However, research on sleep shows that most people need 7 to 8 hours of proper sleep for optimum health and functioning. I personally need around 7.5 - 8 hours of sleep. When I sleep properly, I feel refreshed and energized all day.

Try getting up at different times in the morning to find your unique sleep requirement. You would eventually end up somewhere between 7 to 8:30 hours. Whatever your need is, get that many hours of sleep every day.

Don't be afraid of losing your productivity time. Some people think sleeping 8 hours is a waste of time. Actually, you will be a LOT more productive the whole day. You will get much more done. That one hour of extra sleep will result in several hours of increased performance during the day. It's a worthy trade-off.

One more thing. It's not just the quantity of sleep that is important. "Quality" is also critical. Search online about improving the quality of your sleep. A lot of good information is available. Use that to your advantage.

Note: Please consult your physician before making any changes in your diet, exercise, or lifestyle. Each one of us has our own unique physical and mental condition and benefit from more personalized advice. The pointers given above are general guidelines for good health, but professional medical advice should always be your priority.

Try switching to healthy food and notice the difference in your thought process. You will be pleasantly surprised. And if you continue with this diet over the long term, you will have better health and a strong immune system to boot.

Parting Thoughts

You have just learned several powerful ideas and tools to build an unshakable, rock-solid sense of positivity. These are some of my most cherished pieces of information on building an optimistic personality. I have extensively used these to change my thought process from negative to a positive one.

Now it's up to you to take this knowledge and use it wisely. Remember: without its application, knowledge has no value. But when acted upon, it has the power to change our destiny.

Use this information well, and it will continue to serve you forever.

I wish you all the happiness, love, and success that you truly deserve.

Vishal Pandey.

Let me know your thoughts.

I want to know what you are thinking. Your thoughts and ideas are important to me. I would be grateful if you'd post a short review on Amazon. Your support makes a significant difference. I read all reviews myself so that I can gather your feedback and make improvements to the book.

Your support is deeply appreciated!

About The Author

After completing post-graduation in business management, Vishal Pandey joined the corporate world, only to realize that it was not the path for him. His decade-old passion for self-development led him to the world of writing and the creation of his blog.

Over the course of sixteen years, he read hundreds of books, listened to audio/video programs, attended seminars on the topic of personal development, and tested every piece of information by applying it in real life.

His blog was originally created to share this information with the world but later evolved into a platform for mutual interaction with his readers. After receiving several requests to write a book from his readers, he wrote 'Positive Thinking,' 'Success Habits of High Achievers,' and 'The Power of Positive Energy.'

Besides writing, he loves meditation, yoga, martial arts, music, nutrition, psychology, human behavior, and traveling.

You can contact him at:

Email: yourselfactualization@gmail.com

Facebook: facebook.com/selfactualization.co

Twitter: @selfactualized9

More Books by Vishal Pandey

Made in the USA
Middletown, DE
04 September 2021